CENTRALIZATION
AND DECENTRALIZATION IN
INDUSTRIAL RELATIONS

CENTRALIZATION AND DECENTRALIZATION IN INDUSTRIAL RELATIONS

By
Helen Baker, *Associate Director*
and
Robert R. France, *Research Associate*
Industrial Relations Section

1954
INDUSTRIAL RELATIONS SECTION
DEPARTMENT OF ECONOMICS AND SOCIOLOGY
PRINCETON UNIVERSITY, PRINCETON, NEW JERSEY

INDUSTRIAL RELATIONS SECTION
DEPARTMENT OF ECONOMICS AND SOCIOLOGY
PRINCETON UNIVERSITY
Established 1922

J. Douglas Brown, Director
Helen Baker, Associate Director
Hazel C. Benjamin, Librarian

━━━━━━

Richard A. Lester, Research Associate
Robert R. France, Research Associate
Sherrill Cleland, Research Assistant
Werner Blumenthal, Research Assistant

The reports of the Industrial Relations Section are the joint product of the Section's staff under the supervision of the Director. In the case of each report, the research and preparation of manuscript is done by the staff members whose names appear on the title page.

Research Report Series: No. 87

FOREWORD

IN the perspective of history, the large multiplant corporation is a recent social invention which still faces years of evolution in meeting the problems of size, distance, inertia and initiative. Its powers of adaptation to new and varied conditions will be constantly tested in a period of dynamic growth. Not the least of these tests will be that of the response of the people who work for a corporation whose center of authority may be a thousand miles away. It is safe to say that such large and complex organizations will prosper in our political and social climate only if we learn to operate them in a way which human beings can understand and respect, not only in terms of law and economics, but also in their emotions and motivations.

The problems of human organizations of great size and spread are by no means confined to industrial corporations. They have long been met in governments, churches, and commercial associations. History is full of the accounts of the successes and failures of empires, hierarchies, and trading companies in expanding and consolidating their control over distant areas, populations, and memberships. Despite sharp distinctions in purpose, a common problem in all such human organizations is the dichotomy between the pressure for *centralization* of authority to assure *corporate integrity*, and the countering pressure for *decentralization* in administration to secure *efficiency* through ready response to diverse conditions and human motivations. While the events of history may not repeat themselves, the human reactions which bring them about seem to persist through time.

In the modern industrial corporation, the reasons for seeking decentralization in administration are numerous and readily explained. The executives of many large American companies have given a great deal of attention to this aspect of the dichotomy in corporate pressures. The reasons for centralization in authority, however, involve factors which are less tangible than day-to-day efficiency and more subtle in their long-run influence upon the corporation. Integrity in a corporation, like in an individual, relates to a whole system of behaviour which is only apparent over time. It involves far more than specific standards of behaviour like honesty. It is the attribute of "oneness" in character and personality. It is the requisite of the social momentum of a corporate tradition, of continuity in relationships not fixed by law, of established respect in the community, and of sustained loyalty on the part of those who are employed. Corporate personality is what people think a corporation *is* apart from its changing executive leadership. It can become disintegrated—schizophrenic—and deteriorate slowly but surely over the years.

It is probably in the industrial relations aspects of corporate operations that the dichotomy of centralization and decentralization has become most apparent in the large, multiplant organization. In industrial relations, the appeal of ready adjustment of policies and administration to local groups and local conditions is great. Human beings respond quickly to leadership which can be seen and known. But in no aspect of corporate policy is continuity and consistency of corporate personality—integrity—more important than in industrial relations. No matter how effective on a plant-by-plant basis, the corporation which seeks to prosper through the years cannot be all things to all men. It must earn the substantial respect and loyalty of all groups in its employ by policies which prevail throughout its operations. Such policies and their equitable application are the evidences of the "oneness" of the corporation and an assurance to the career employee that he is related to something more than a changing stream of men.

Because of the fundamental nature of this problem of balancing the pressures for centralization and for decentralization in corporate policy and its special significance in the area of industrial relations, the Industrial Relations Section undertook in 1952 a thorough study of the problem. The ready response of a large number of companies to our inquiries gave confirmation that the problem was of practical as well as fundamental importance. The Section is most grateful to the company and union representatives who cooperated so generously in giving their time and thought to the study.

Miss Helen Baker, Associate Director of the Section, who has directed the study, has been assisted throughout by Robert R. France, Research Associate in the Section and Assistant Professor of Economics. Professor France is the author of Chapters III and V. Dr. Otto Lerbinger, formerly Research Assistant, worked with the project from September, 1952 through November, 1953. He conducted many interviews, assisted in the analysis of findings, and prepared preliminary drafts of three chapters. In addition, six second-year graduate students of the Woodrow Wilson School of Public and International Affairs of the University participated in the project in partial fulfillment of degree requirements. They were: D. Carlisle Black, Jr., W. Michael

Blumenthal, James E. Bradshaw, James Theodore Harris, Jr., Karl E. Meyer, and Gerald A. Pollack. Their help in the field work made possible a considerable expansion of the program of interviews.

J. Douglas Brown
Director

Princeton, New Jersey
August 18, 1954

CONTENTS

INTRODUCTION AND BACKGROUND
SITUATION

I. INTRODUCTION

CHANGING opinions and attitudes are often revealed in the increased use of a word. What was once a simple descriptive term may become a watchword, fraught with emotion and value connotations. Such seems to have been the case with *decentralized management*. Decentralization has come to mean not just a movement away from centralization but improved industrial organization, efficient operations, and forward-looking management. More often than not it has been used to imply all-out decentralization, without differentiation in its practical application to different management functions. Goals frequently have been as broad as "to make each plant completely autonomous," or "to make each plant manager act as if he were running his own business," even though it has also been pointed out that "decentralization stated in extreme terms is ridiculous and impracticable."

The stated goals of decentralization and reported experience in companies in which the goals were being effectuated through major changes in the organization structure have not often dealt directly with industrial relations. Yet, evidently, a company's organization for industrial relations can be affected by the change in the total organizational structure, and its personnel and labor policies influenced by a company-wide acceptance of the desirability of decentralization.

Discussions with a number of industrial relations executives prior to the beginning of this study revealed that new emphasis on decentralization resulted in certain dilemmas between the goals for decentralization and those sought in the development and application of industrial relations policies. Some awareness of these dilemmas had begun to raise questions as to the extent to which decentralization could or should be applied to industrial relations. At the same time, personnel managers expressed hope and confidence that decentralization might help in a number of ways to improve management-employee relationships. There was, apparently, little effort to appraise the soundness of these hopes in the light of observed problems and dilemmas.

A. OBJECTIVES OF THE STUDY

Preliminary interviews served to underline the fact that decentralization cannot be studied alone, since it exists only in relation to centralization. The important questions for study, it was evident, were related to degree and balance rather than to the pros and cons of extreme decentralization. The subject of study is, therefore, not "decentralization" but "centralization and decentralization of the industrial relations function."

The broad purpose of this study grew out of the observed need for a clearer understanding of the impact that efforts to achieve a greater decentralization of general management have on one important function of management—industrial relations. Six specific objectives were set up:

1. To examine the objectives of and attitudes towards decentralization of the industrial relations function as compared with decentralization in general management.

2. To determine the extent of present decentralization in the industrial relations function as compared with present decentralization in general management and with past practice in industrial relations administration.

3. To identify and evaluate the relative importance of factors influencing an industrial organization towards more or less decentralization of its industrial relations function.

4. To study the relationship of centralization and decentralization to methods of coordination and control in industrial relations administration.

5. To gather and evaluate opinion and evidence of the effect of the degree of centralization and decentralization upon—

a. Intra-management relations
b. Supervisory and executive competency and growth
c. Employee-management relations
d. Union-management relations
e. Total organizational effectiveness

6. To determine the factors essential to attainment of the optimum degree of decentralization.

The sixth original objective was dropped when in the course of interviewing it became clear that the balance between centralization and decentralization was variable among all the different sub-functions of industrial relations. A list of "factors essential to attainment of the optimum degree of decentralization" could serve no useful purpose if no optimum degree of decentralization of the industrial relations function as a whole were possible.

B. Scope and Methods

A study of centralization and decentralization in the industrial relations function clearly required investigation of the allocation of respon-

sibility for this function among the principal levels of management—
the corporation, the subsidiary, division, or product department, and
the plant. Thus the nature of the study required that the companies to
be included should be multiplant. It was also necessary, if there was
to be any appraisal of the depth of decentralization and of its impact
and problems at the operating level, to study the extent of delegation
within the levels of plant management.[1]

The method of investigation,[2] it was decided, should be a combination of questionnairing and interviewing, both to be used in connection
with all of the companies cooperating in the study. This plan was later
modified to include a special letter to the president and a short questionnaire to the industrial relations executive of certain companies in which
no interviews were sought. It was also decided that any attempted appraisal of the extent or impact of decentralization on labor relations
must take into account union opinion. Consequently, interviews were
sought with officers of the principal national unions representing the
employees of the companies interviewed and with representatives of
the local unions negotiating with the plants covered in the case studies.

The heart of the study was seen to be in the information and opinions
received from selected multiplant companies by questionnaire and by
interviews at the corporation level (the "survey" companies), and in
the information and opinions received from four multiplant companies in
which extensive and intensive interviews were held at corporation, division, and plant levels (the "case study" companies). Supplementary to
that material were the letters from chief executives of companies giving
their opinions concerning the desirable extent of decentralization in
general management and industrial relations, the short questionnaire,
and reports of interviews with union representatives.

The number of companies from which information was received
totalled 135, divided as follows:

Case studies	4
Survey companies	42
Letters from a chief executive or his representative and/or responses to short questionnaire	89

The number of employees in the 42 survey companies was, as of
December, 1952, approximately 2,100,000, in the four case studies,
140,000, and in the 89 companies from which letters and/or short ques-

---

[1] A supplementary report, "Delegation of Responsibility for Industrial Relations within
the Plant," will provide a more detailed discussion of this aspect of decentralization.

[2] See Appendices for questionnaire forms and further discussion of methods.

tionnaires were received 1,260,000, making a total of three and a half million employees in all of the cooperating companies. The survey companies ranged in number of employees from 3,000 to over 200,000; the four case studies from 500 to 90,000; and the 89 companies from 2,200 to 76,000. The median number of employees per company was near 20,000. The number of plants per company in the survey and case study group ranged from 4 to over 200 with a median of 17, and in the 89 companies from 3 to 32 with a median of 7.

By no standard can any but one case study company be considered a small company. No claim is made as to the representativeness of the sample although the employees, as of 1952, in the 134 manufacturing companies were approximately 20 per cent of the average number employed in manufacturing in 1952. Nevertheless it is felt that the group as a whole covers the principal facets of executive opinion on, and headquarters experience with, centralization and decentralization of the industrial relations function in multiplant companies in the United States, and that interviews in the nine plants of the four case studies give substantial insights into the extent and effects of centralization and decentralization upon industrial relations in operating units.

The distribution of the 42 survey and four case study companies by industry, number of plants, and number of employees is shown in Table 1. Many of the larger companies represented more than one industry. These companies were listed for inclusion in Table 1 only under the one industry which was most generally representative of the company's products. The total number of major industries represented in all of the 135 companies from which information was received totalled 25.

C. Definitions

Definitions are an important preliminary consideration in a study dealing with words that have different meanings in different contexts and are often subject to controversy. One study or one organization cannot impose its own usage upon others, but it can define terms for the purpose of the study with due consideration for common usage and then attempt to use them consistently throughout. Such an effort has been made especially with respect to the following words or phrases.

1. *Decentralization* is used in this study only in relation to administrative decentralization, and is specifically defined as the minimization of decision making at the highest, central point of authority and the maximization of the delegation of responsibility and authority in the making of decisions to lower levels of management. Administrative

TABLE 1. DISTRIBUTION OF 46 COMPANIES BY INDUSTRY, NUMBER OF PLANTS, AND NUMBER OF EMPLOYEES

Industry	Number of Plants				Number of Employees					Totals by industry
	5 or under	6-20	21-50	Over 50	Under 1,000	1,000-4,999	5,000-19,999	20,000-49,999	50,000 and over	
Manufacturing										
Automobile				1					1	2
Building materials	1	3			1					4
Chemicals	2	1	1	2		2	2	1	1	6
Electrical machinery and electrical and scientific instruments	1	4		1		3	1	1	1	6
Food	1	1		1			3			3
Heavy machinery		2	2			1	1	1	1	4
Paper		3					3			3
Petroleum		5	1	1			2	4	1	7
Rubber		3	2				1	1	3	5
Steel and other metals and metal products		1	1	2			1	2	1	4
Textiles		1					1			1
Merchandising				1					1	1
Totals by number of plants and number of employees	5	24	8	9	1	6	16	13	10	46
		46					46			

decentralization is not to be confused with geographical decentralization of the operating units of an organization.

The level of decision making is the crux of this definition. As will be seen in many of the following chapters, it cannot always be ascertained who is involved in the making of a specific decision. However, the point at which action is determined is a fact which can be isolated in formal decision making and at least located as to area in informal decision making.

2. *Industrial relations function.* Industrial relations is used in its broadest sense to include both personnel administration and labor relations. The list of specific activities to be included in the "industrial relations function" was compiled carefully on the basis of general texts in this field and previous studies of the Industrial Relations Section, and after consultation with industrial relations officers with whom methods and scope of the study were discussed. The 21 activities or sub-functions on which information was sought[1] were later combined, for the presentation of findings, into four principal groups: (1) manpower maintenance; (2) wages, salaries, and hours; (3) pension and benefit plans; and (4) management-union relations.

3. *Policy* is used to include not only the very broad statements of company intent, but also those parts of plans and agreements that establish the pattern or "laws" for a consistent, long-term course of action.

4. *Implementation of policy* refers to parts of plans or other procedures that specify in detail how a policy is to be applied.

5. *Application of policy* is used with reference to specific decisions concerned with the individual situation or person. Such specific decisions include both those made within the limits of established policy and procedure and those made or initiated at lower management levels when no guiding policy has been established.

6. *Coordination* is defined for this study as the process of ensuring that centrally determined policy will be uniformly applied and that, in making decisions in any one unit, management personnel will take into account the possible impact on other units and on the corporation as a whole.

7. *Control,* as discussed in Chapter V, is used in the technical sense of audit or review of the application of industrial relations policies and established procedures.

Some of the special problems in a study of centralization and decentralization of the industrial relations function may be observed in the

[1] See Appendix A.

above definitions. "Industrial relations" when used synonomously with "human relations in industry" was often found to refer not so much to the determination, implementation, or application of policy as to the condition of person-to-person relationships. "Delegation" was found to cover not only a specifically defined area of responsibility, but also the following variations: (1) general assignment of responsibility with specific policy limitations; (2) general assignment carrying with it the need both to be informed on relevant facts and to consult a higher echelon prior to decision; and (3) an undefinable "plus" in addition to the general or specific assignment that is implied in the terms "reaching out" and "stewardship."

The formal structure for and procedures in decision making had to be accepted as the basic facts in the findings. However, informal and tenuous objectives and procedures had also to be considered if the conclusions to be drawn from the findings were to be realistic. The following chapters thus are the result of an attempted synthesis of all that was reported as to clearly stated or just-being-thought-out objectives and policies, and as to formal and informal procedures, and of supplementary documentary material and observation of fact.

II. CURRENT MANAGEMENT ATTITUDES TOWARD CENTRALIZATION AND DECENTRALIZATION

TWO points became clear from the preliminary interviews with chief industrial relations officers and from the first intensive interviews on a case study basis: (1) decentralization, as a principle, is widely accepted by all levels of management without much critical appraisal of its actual practice or its possible impact; (2) centralization or decentralization of the industrial relations function can be evaluated only with considerable knowledge of the attitudes of top management towards centralization and decentralization as applied both in general management and in the particular function being studied. Consequently information was sought on attitudes and reasons for them as well as on practices and problems.

A letter to company presidents asked two questions:

"Do you favor a higher degree of centralization or decentralization of your company than now exists?

"Do you favor more or less centralization of the industrial relations function than of management functions generally?"[1]

Direct replies to these questions were received from 57 presidents or other top executives. Nineteen industrial relations executives, in addition, replied for their chief executive. The four "case studies" and the 42 companies in which interviews were held with the headquarters industrial relations staff also supplied information on attitudes as well as insight into reasons for a preference for more or less decentralization.

The attitudes shown in interviews and letters are reported in this chapter. Drawing on the four case studies as well as the more limited company interviews and correspondence, an attempt is made in the last section of this chapter to appraise the extent of decentralization practiced among the reporting companies compared with the strength of opinion favorable to it.

[1] Excerpts are put in quotation marks if they are exact quotations. Excerpts are not set in quotation marks if taken from interview records in which the statement of the interviewee may have been paraphrased in any respect.

A. Opinions of Chief Executives

1. *Towards centralization or decentralization of general management*

Top executive opinion is strongly favorable to decentralization of general management. The statements of a majority of the industrial relations managers replying for a chief executive also reveal a similar preference. It is interesting to note, however, that, as a group, these heads of staff were less favorable than their superiors to a high degree of decentralization and considerably more favorable to centralization or to a variable balance depending on changing circumstances. Table 2

TABLE 2. OPINIONS RELATIVE TO CENTRALIZATION OR
DECENTRALIZATION OF GENERAL MANAGEMENT

Opinion Favoring	% of 57 replies from top executives	% of 19 ind. rels. officers replying for a chief executive	% of 76 replies from top execs. and ind. rels. officers
Continuing high degree of decentralization	47.4 ⎱ 73.7	42 ⎱ 58	46 ⎱ 70
Higher degree of decentralization than now	26.3 ⎰	16 ⎰	24 ⎰
High degree of centralization	7	10.5	8
Variable balance	19.3	31.5	22

shows the results of an analysis of the replies directly from top executives and from industrial relations officers replying for a chief executive, and of the total replies received in response to the letter to company presidents.

The impressive total of almost 75 per cent of the top management personnel replying favorably to decentralization covers a great variety of individual company situations. An outstanding circumstance reported both by those having a presently satisfactory degree of decentralization and those seeking a higher degree is that developments in this direction are of recent date. For example, among the former group were such statements as:

"——————— Company has been decentralizing its general operations for the past five years. We have found this move has been a sound one, and we're enjoying much better administration as a result."

Representative comments from those favoring a higher degree of decentralization than they now have in general operations were:

"My objective concerning the general management in ————
Corporation is that of a small corporate staff composed of relatively
few, highly competent individuals with a maximum degree of delegation to experienced and trained managers of our geographically widely
separated operating (manufacturing) divisions. This objective, of
course, can be realized only as rapidly as corporate staff and division
personnel are adequately trained to assume the type of responsibility
indicated. Therefore, you might say that, from the standpoint of management philosophy, I favor a lesser degree of centralization than has
been characteristic of [the company] in its more recent past but feel
that the process of decentralization is a gradual one."

"For many years past we have been working toward greater decentralization in the general management of our Company. This planned
program was based upon the belief, subsequently verified by experience,
that many advantages accrue and the end result of such program is
more effective operation. We have achieved this greater decentralization through the means of granting increased authority—monetary and
otherwise—to management. At times our decentralization has taken the
form of establishing subsidiary companies because of geographical or
other specialized need.

"We believe we have gone far in achieving decentralized general
management with centralized guidance and appraisal of results. I do
not believe we have reached the optimum in this direction. For example,
we are currently studying our top organization with the objective of
further freeing our officer level executives from day-to-day operating
decisions."

A letter from one executive favoring a high degree of centralization
for general management illustrates the attitude of a number of others
that what is best for one company is not necessarily best for another.

"It is our opinion that this subject could be argued for a long period
of time and the results would be no one system would adequately fit
all types of industry. . . . In our own particular case, we are fairly
confident that a strong central general management is necessary to
coordinate our financial, manufacturing and selling endeavors."

The companies classified as "favoring a variable balance" were different from those in the other three classes in that they felt it was impractical to aim for a high degree of either centralization or decentralization. They were of the opinion not only that no two companies faced
identical circumstances, but that, of even more importance, the desirable
or possible degree of decentralization varied from time to time, from

function to function, and from plant to plant. The following are typical expressions of this point of view among chief executives:

"Our present degree of centralization or decentralization is considered satisfactory in relation to conditions as now existing. The degree of decentralization varies from one operating unit to another depending on the size of the unit, the type and capacity of local management, the proximity of the unit, the operating problems involved and other factors. Also, as might be expected, decentralization varies considerably from one function to another. The degree of centralization has been revised from time to time because of changing conditions and operating experience. Further revisions will undoubtedly be made in the future, though no major change is contemplated at present."

"I generally feel that I can make no definite choice as to the two extremes. If the question were applied to specific function and department, I might have definite points of view concerning the degree of centralization or decentralization. Generally, our policy is to give a man sufficient authority to perform his responsibilities; and depending on the particular job that he occupies, it may be wholly centralized or wholly decentralized."

An industrial relations director replied in similar vein:

"The degree of centralized control existing with respect to any particular function depends to a large degree upon the necessity for close coordination and uniformity among the various branches. For example, it is obviously necessary to have uniform accounting practices and procedures. On the other hand, other functions, such as purchasing . . . , lend themselves more readily to and can be more effective if a greater degree of decentralization exists."

2. Opinion as to relative degree of decentralization for general management and for the industrial relations function

The principal points of interest in Table 3 are the substantial minority opinion that a higher degree of centralization is desirable for the industrial relations function than for management functions generally, and the small percentage of companies that see the need for greater decentralization for industrial relations. Only eight chief executives and not one industrial relations officer favored a higher degree of decentralization for industrial relations than for general management. This is an important fact to bear in mind in comparing the findings of this study which deals only with the industrial relations function with other more general studies of decentralization.

TABLE 3. THE RELATIVE DEGREE OF CENTRALIZATION OR
DECENTRALIZATION DESIRED FOR GENERAL MANAGEMENT AND FOR
THE INDUSTRIAL RELATIONS FUNCTION

Opinions Favoring	% of 57 replies by chief execs.	% of 19 replies by ind. rels. officers	% of total of 76 replies	
Same degrees for both, and also favoring	51	58		52.7
Decentralized general management	39	32	37	
Centralized general management	3	5		3.8
A variable balance	9	21		11.9
Greater centralization for industrial relations than for general management, and also favoring	35	42		36.8
Decentralization for general management	26	26	26.3	
Centralized general management	—	—		—
Variable balance	9	16		10.5
Greater decentralization for industrial relations, and also favoring	14			10.5
Decentralized general management	9		6.6	
Centralized general management	3		2.6	
Variable balance	2		1.3	

B. OPINIONS OF INDUSTRIAL RELATIONS SPECIALISTS

The opinions that were secured from industrial relations specialists in personal interviews tended to be more complex than the statements given in letters. Nevertheless there was one common characteristic in a large majority of the responses. The head of the industrial relations staff tended in his first comments to reflect the company point of view which was predominantly favorable to decentralization. As the discussion continued he showed his awareness that many industrial relations activities were highly centralized and his own belief that the possibility of greater decentralization depended on many variable factors.

The following instances are examples of this common reaction:

The personnel director of one company whose first reply was "Our management favors decentralization. This has been a development of the past ten years," later stated:

> Centralization and decentralization are always a matter of degree. . . . Outlying managements are eager to know what headquarters wants them to do. . . . Yet personnel policies, to be satisfactory, must be adjusted to local conditions. Different elements in the local situation must be balanced against corporation objectives and policies. Success in this balancing process is much more important than the degree of centralization or decentralization.

Another industrial relations manager first stressed the company philosophy of decentralization and quoted a company report stating that plant managers are just as responsible for personnel relations as they are for operations. He went on, then, to point out that the amount of autonomy allowed each division and plant depended on many things such as

> how long a man has been plant manager, the product, and whether it is a recently established plant. . . . There is no basic conflict between uniformly high standards in industrial relations and the delegation of more responsibility to the plants, but it takes continuous hard work to reconcile the two.

Other interviews revealed greater conflicts in the personnel officer's own thinking. For example, a member of one company's headquarters industrial relations staff began by saying that the corporation was highly decentralized and that its operating units were "as autonomous as if they were separate, independent companies." Soon this generalization was modified by the statement that "one had to assume that there were certain limiting circumstances" and that "obviously major personnel policies must have the further approval of top management." Later this staff officer made the distinction between policies that should be established on a corporation-wide basis and those that could be determined locally. Finally he described certain activities in which the application of policy was chiefly the responsibility of the headquarters staff and referred to one program for which, in his opinion, more direct central guidance and control were needed.

In a few instances, the original statement of preference for a generally high degree of decentralization turned out to be concerned primarily with collective bargaining. According to one vice president, for example, he and the top officers of the company were so convinced of the desirability of bargaining on a local level that they had decided to permit the negotiation of separate pension plans rather than bargain with the international union over revisions in the one plan now covering all the hourly workers of the company. He agreed that there would continue to be a substantial amount of central decision making in such an arrangement. He also reported with approval the central initiation and direct handling of certain other personnel activities. However, the area-of-bargaining issue was of such importance, in his opinion, that decentralization of industrial relations should be as extensive as possible in order to strengthen the plant managers in their dealings with labor.

It is an interesting fact that the few industrial relations directors who expressed a strong preference for centralization also seemed to be influenced largely by labor relations.

Taking into account opinions as to the desirable level of decision making for the total group of activities in industrial relations, not one of the specialists interviewed was in favor of a high degree of either centralization or decentralization for the industrial relations function as a whole. Whatever their philosophical bias for or against decentralization, their experience had convinced them that centralization and decentralization are not always important considerations in certain activities. They tended to believe, rather, that the extent of delegation should depend on the objectives of the activity and on whether or not delegation impeded or facilitated their attainment.

C. REASONS FOR EXECUTIVE PREFERENCE FOR CENTRALIZATION OR DECENTRALIZATION

1. *In general management*

Many companies recently reorganized in such a way as to delegate greater authority to divisional levels indicated that improved industrial relations was not a primary consideration in the move toward decentralization. On the contrary, the impact of the organizational change on the industrial relations function sometimes was not even taken into account in advance of the change, a fact commented on a bit ruefully by a few industrial relations directors. The common factor in most of the reasons given for having sought or still seeking a higher degree of decentralization for general operations was increasing size of the corporation.

The principal reasons cited by top executives for a preference for decentralization of general management were:

(1) Increase in size of corporation.

(2) Increase in number of industries represented in the corporation's products.

(3) Increase in number of plants with an accompanying policy of geographical decentralization.

(4) To reduce the decision-making burden of top management, and to give more time for planning.

(5) To permit greater accountability by division.

(6) To facilitate daily operations by prompt on-the-spot decisions.

(7) To facilitate adjustment to local conditions.

(8) To "develop men faster."

The trend towards divisional organization accompanying the growth of corporations is itself a factor in decentralization. Delegation of decision making for production and sales and certain staff functions to the division heads is important in relieving the chief executive of an almost unbearable load of work. However, if real delegation goes no further than the second line of command, it may make little difference to the plant managers and their subordinates. The companies seeking improved daily operations by on-the-spot decisions, closer plant-community relations, and the more rapid development of management personnel were looking towards a deeper delegation of authority.

The three principal reasons given for a preference for centralization of general management were the greater economy in many staff functions (especially in case of many small branch plants), the greater flexibility and speed in decision making, and the belief that "a strong central general management is needed to coordinate our financial, manufacturing, and selling endeavors." Since increasing size is apparently a factor in the general popularity of decentralization it is worth noting that the few companies stating a preference for centralized general management ranged in number of employees from 2,000 to 18,000 as compared with a range of from 500 to over 100,000 for those favoring more decentralization.

2. Reasons for seeking a different degree of centralization or decentralization in general management and in the industrial relations function

a. Favoring greater centralization for industrial relations

As reported in Table 3,[1] a substantial minority of the responding chief executives were of the opinion that greater centralization was desirable for the industrial relations function than for management as

1 See p. 28.

a whole. Their reasons for this difference were similar to the industrial relations specialists' reasons for preferring a higher degree of centralization in industrial relations. A few individuals in both groups viewed decentralization as a sound principle for industrial relations as well as for general management. Many others, however, were reporting from their own experience in pointing out the difficulties of adhering to such a principle. They had found that the possible extent of delegation of authority for a specific function depends more upon given circumstances than upon a general philosophy of organization.

The following include both aims sought in having a high degree of centralization in industrial relations and conditions that require such centralization:

(1) To insure that industrial relations matters receive the attention they should have throughout a corporation, the center of authority must be near the top. Important decisions should be made by executives responsible for the corporation as a whole, and the central industrial relations staff should be in a position to advise top management as well as its operating divisions.

(2) Uniformity of industrial relations policies and their application is needed to give employees a sense of being treated fairly. When provisions of a multiplant labor contract are involved, uniform interpretation is essential. Even when a company has contracts with several unions, or none, uniformity is desirable except for instances in which local custom may be of controlling interest to the employees of a given plant.

(3) Aside from the question of uniformity, central clearance of many industrial relations decisions made by local managers is essential to avoid unexpected repercussions in other plants. Decisions in one division often have an impact on the same or even an unrelated activity in another division because of a combination of circumstances that is visible only to someone acquainted with both units of operation.

(4) Sudden changes in labor relations require quick decisions by management. Greater flexibility is insured when decisions are made by a few officers who have frequent informal contacts.

(5) Central handling of labor relations is accepted as a condition of multiplant bargaining, but it was frequently stated that centralization is equally important to avoid "whipsawing" when local bargaining prevails.

(6) Labor legislation and government intervention in labor relations require central administration or control to insure maintenance of legal standards and adequate legal counsel throughout the corporation.

(7) As a matter of economy, certain special staff services (such as legal and actuarial advice) are located only in the head office.

(8) Plant managers and supervisors find it more of "a mental strain" to make decisions in labor and personnel relations than in technical matters. Even when nominally responsible for industrial relations in his unit of operations, the plant manager or supervisor likes to be able to "clear" with the industrial relations manager or a higher line executive before making any but the most minor decisions.

b. Favoring greater decentralization for industrial relations

Three principal reasons were given by the few companies favoring greater decentralization for the industrial relations function than for general management:

(1) Industrial relations problems are handled most effectively on the basis of local conditions.

(2) Since responsibility for dealing with people is an inseparable part of line management, employee relations should be handled as near the level of first line supervision as possible.

(3) In some cases the nature of a company's products makes it especially desirable to maintain a friendly relationship with the communities in which its plants are located. This objective, in the opinion of one company, "can be achieved only by decentralization of a number of industrial relations functions."

3. Belief in need for a variable balance between centralization and decentralization

Those companies seeing the need for a variable balance between centralization and decentralization have pointed out not only that conditions vary between companies but also that conditions may change frequently within a given company. The factors that are believed to indicate the need for more or less centralization are related to the character of the organization, the location of its plants, the qualifications and personalities of management personnel, and outside conditions that influence company policies.[1] An officer of one company stressed the fact that the process of change itself requires a high degree of centralization until the new elements become a part of accepted routines and relationships.

Most executives commenting on the need for balance spoke in terms

[1] These factors are discussed in relation to the total industrial relations function in Chapter IV and in relation to specific industrial relations functions in Chapters VI-IX.

of the practical necessity for continual adjustment to changing circumstance. Only a few had a strong opinion as to the desirability of frequent change on the one hand or a long-time stable balance on the other. The following comments illustrate these opposite points of view:

"I believe there will be a continuous swing of the pendulum and feel these changes are for the good. Change upsets rigid bureaucracies and relationships and develops more flexible managers."

"The goal of management with respect to decentralization and centralization should be one of balance as should also the matter of line and staff responsibility. . . . The real secret of successful business is to avoid the hazards of extremes. It is dangerous to change rapidly from centralization to decentralization and back again."

A careful appraisal of opinions and reported experience suggests that successful compromise between these two points of view is important. The desirable goal would seem to be to provide the satisfaction of stable relationships through the type of leadership and coordination that would also prevent "rigid bureaucracies" and assure intelligent response to changing situations.

D. Management Attitudes Compared with Company Practice

1. *Comparison of attitudes and practice*

The outstanding impression gained from a review of management opinions and reported practice is the discrepancy betwen the widespread company philosophy of decentralization and common practice with respect to delegation of responsibility for specific industrial relations activities.[1] Top management philosophy, as reported above, was overwhelmingly favorable to decentralization. The original response of more than half of the industrial relations executives interviewed also indicated a preference for decentralization. Yet an analysis of the levels of decision making for industrial relations policies and procedures revealed a marked tendency towards centralization.

In measuring the degree of centralization or decentralization, the level of decision making was considered for policy decisions and for procedural decisions (that is, related to the implementation and application of policies) for 21 specific industrial relations activities.[2] As far as policy determination is concerned, decisions are predominantly at

[1] See Chapters VI-IX.
[2] See Chapter IV for more detailed discussion of location of general responsibility for the industrial relations function, Chapters VI to IX for discussion of practice in specific sub-functions or activities, and Appendix B for a description of methods.

the corporate level. Only in case of a very few items, such as non-supervisory promotions and training, were policies permitted to be made at the plant level in as many as 35 per cent of the reporting companies. For 17 of the 21 activities, policies were established at the corporate level in from 80 to 100 per cent of these companies.

As was commonly reported, matters of procedure were handled more frequently at the division or plant level. But for a majority of the activities (13 out of 21) exact procedures in applying the policy were, in a majority of the companies, developed at headquarters. Moreover, interviews among plant management personnel indicated that supervisors' and even the plant manager's discretion is narrowly limited in the application of policy as well as in its determination. Questions of interpretation of company policy or of the labor contract were found to be settled in most of the companies at the top level of plant management after consultation with division or headquarters staff. The industrial relations responsibility of the supervisor is primarily the maintenance of satisfactory person-to-person relationships under given policies and given procedures—not the making of important decisions. Such a relationship is the essence of successful supervision; but does it in itself constitute decentralization?

2. *Some reasons for the discrepancy between attitudes and practice*

Many of the executives providing information were aware of the discrepancy between their company's general philosophy of decentralization and industrial relations practice. Interviews brought forth strong comments on the difference between philosophy and practice. Some of the heads of industrial relations staffs felt that, in spite of lip service to decentralization, there was frequent failure on the part of both line and staff to "work hard at delegation." One personnel director was of the opinion that, until recently, his company's philosophy of decentralization had been but "a pious hope" as far as personnel administration was concerned. Another stated that he was sure the officers of the company sincerely believed in decentralization but that generally they did not know how to delegate.

These comments on the discrepancy between the desired and the actual degree of decentralization suggested, directly or by implication, reasons for the existing difference. Expressed in many forms, they may be categorized as follows:

(1) The statement of decentralization as a philosophy or principle of organization is a *goal* rather than a description of *current practice*.

Many of the company statements reflected the idea that "a man's reach should exceed his grasp." Because even limited decentralization, according to these opinions, is more satisfactory than extreme centralization, decentralization should be stated repeatedly as a goal. The more it is talked about, the more all levels of management personnel will be encouraged to delegate and to exercise judgment in matters for which they are responsible.

(2) The word "decentralization" is used in many ways, and company executives stating a preference for "decentralized management" may not mean extensive delegation of authority to make decisions. Geographical decentralization of plants is sometimes confused with administrative decentralization. Decentralization may be viewed only in connection with headquarters-division or headquarters-plant relationships with no specific encouragement of delegation of responsibility for industrial relations to lower levels of management. Where there once had been a very high degree of centralization, the change in trend may seem more significant than the presently attained extent or depth of delegation.

The wide interest in improved communications and wider participation in planning may result in these activities being looked upon as forms of decentralization since such practices have often been given new emphasis with greater interest in decentralization. And, finally, some executives considered decentralization primarily as a matter of the satisfactory handling of person-to-person relationships by lower levels of management.

(3) Dilemmas in the conflicting goals of decentralization and effective industrial relations are not easy to resolve. Many companies sincerely seeking the benefits of managerial decentralization still find it very difficult to delegate responsibility for certain industrial relations functions. The peculiar need for integrated corporation policies in personnel and labor relations, the risks involved in delegating responsibility for major decisions, the frequent desire of middle management and lower levels of supervision to avoid or to share with a higher echelon responsibility in personnel and labor relations, and the advantages of company-wide pension and insurance plans are but a few of the problems that face managements working towards greater delegation of authority to lower levels of management.

(4) Decentralization is a current "fad" which some companies have adopted as a slogan without attempting seriously to put it into action. Criticism of this attitude was most succinctly stated by one executive vice president:

"I find myself just a little annoyed at the tendency of all of us to adopt certain clichés such as 'decentralization' and then glibly announce that we are for it. I have been somewhat amused at some of my colleagues who are most vocal in expounding the virtues of decentralization and yet quite unconsciously are apt to be very busily engaged in developing their own personal control over activities for which they are responsible."

The explanation of the discrepancy between philosophy and practice thus appears to be a compound of hopes and plans not yet fulfilled, of conflicting definitions of "decentralization," of dilemmas in goals, and, in some cases, of adoption of a popular idea without much study of what is involved in its effectuation. Yet many companies are convinced of the great need for and possible benefits from decentralization. Extreme centralization and increasing size have revealed problems in organization, administration, and human relations that make some new approach seem essential. As is often the case when many people are faced with the same problem, a panacea is sought. The following chapters reporting experience and practice in decision making for industrial relations raise serious questions not only as to the present extent of decentralization, but also as to the possibility or desirability of extreme decentralization of the industrial relations function.

III. THE ORGANIZATIONAL STRUCTURE

T HE organizational structure determines formally the limits of authority and the lines along which it is delegated within the firm. Consequently, this structure may have some effect on the level at which decisions on industrial relations matters are made. In an effort to discover any relationships that might exist between the organizational structure and centralization or decentralization, information on company organization was obtained from the firms interviewed.

A. CORPORATE AND DIVISIONAL ORGANIZATION

1. *Line organization*

a. Basis of organization

In recent discussions it has been held that organizing a business along the lines of functional specialization encourages centralization of general management. Individuals in charge of such specialized groups do not have control over all factors of importance in making decisions. Consequently, matters tend to be referred to top level management. Decentralization requires the utilization of integrated sub-units encompassing the essential variables that affect decision making.

The structure of organization thus may have an indirect effect on the level at which decisions are made with respect to industrial relations. If the head of an integrated unit is accustomed to exercising authority for the general management of his operations, he may be more inclined to make his own decisions concerning industrial relations matters than a division head who has had less authority in other areas of management. Emphasis should be given to the indirect nature of this effect, however. It is entirely possible to conceive of situations in which general management is highly decentralized and the industrial relations function highly centralized, and vice versa. For example, it is commonly recognized that perhaps the best known case of decentralization for general management purposes in this country, General Motors, has substantial centralization of the industrial relations function.

The basis of subdivision may have another indirect effect. In many cases, the establishment of corporate divisions on a product basis results from the fabrication in one firm of articles requiring quite diverse processes and technologies. The differences in working conditions resulting may require differentiation in industrial relations matters, particularly in labor relations where the industry pattern may be more important than company policy. Decentralization at least to the division level may thereby be encouraged.

An analysis of the 44 firms providing information in these areas indicates only a weak relationship between the basis of organization and the level of decision making on industrial relations matters. At the corporate level, the closest approximation to integrated units is the product or geographical division. Twenty of the companies are organized along product lines and two along geographic lines. Twenty-two companies are established on a functional basis. All but one of the eight companies in which a significant amount of decision making occurred at the divisional level are organized on the basis of product. However, as indicated in the next section, the fact that in four of the companies the divisions either were, or still are, subsidiary corporations is another contributing factor.

The amount of decision making at the division level does not indicate accurately the degree of centralization or decentralization. As pointed out in Chapter II, if authority is not delegated further to the plants, little decentralization has resulted. On the other hand, the amount of decision making at the divisional level may be small because authority rests with the plants rather than at the division or corporate levels. Of the 22 companies organized on a product or geographical basis, twelve had a significant amount of decision making at the plant level, whereas for the same number of firms organized on a functional basis only eight were classified in that category.

b. Elimination of subsidiaries

The increasing organizational pattern of corporate divisions rather than subsidiary companies also has some effect on the level of decision making. There is evidence that the divisional type of organization is more conducive to centralization than the maintenance of subsidiaries. The elimination of the corporate identity of the subsidiary was felt by a number of executives to strengthen the tendency toward company-wide uniformity in industrial relations policies and to weaken the position of those who felt that historically unique policies should be continued. Furthermore, where most of the officers of the subsidiary company have had long experience in operating as an independent company, the maintenance of the corporate identity of the subsidiary tends to encourage an attitude of independence.

c. Span of control

The span of control is another aspect of the structure of organization which has been discussed along with the basis of subdivision as factors affecting centralization and decentralization of management. The idea has been put forth that a large span of control prevents close supervision and thus encourages decentralization. There was some indication from the relatively little data obtained on this point that the span of control was larger in firms with decentralized industrial relations functions. However, it should be pointed out that by the delegation of line responsibility to industrial relations staffs, executives with large numbers of subordinates reporting to them could maintain centralized authority over industrial relations.

2. *Corporate and divisional industrial relations staffs*

a. Location and size

Of the 46 companies in the group interviewed, all but one had an industrial relations staff at the corporate level. The lone exception was the smallest firm studied, and even in this case, the vice president in charge of manufacturing functioned in that capacity. Of the 44 companies having a divisional level between the plant and the parent corporation, 18 had industrial relations staffs at that intermediary level.

In some ways, the use of divisional staffs encourages decentralization to that level. With its own staff available, divisional line management is no longer required to seek advice from the corporate staff. Divisional staff personnel, concentrating on the peculiar industrial relations problems existing within their division, emphasize the need for different policies to cover the diverse situation in the various operating groups. Thus decision making at the division level is promoted. If communications between divisional and corporate staffs are not fully maintained, either inadvertently or intentionally, increased independence of action for divisional staffs results. Thus one company reported:

> As the situation exists, the divisional industrial relations managers do not always refer problems to the corporate staff which they should. In some cases the corporate staff hears only indirectly about action, which the corporate staff considers poor industrial relations, taken by plant or divisional industrial relations personnel.

However, as indicated in Chapter IV, if the divisional staff emphasizes its role as an agency of the corporate staff, centralization rather than decentralization may be encouraged by the use of divisional staffs. Some of the companies studied, seeking a degree of decentralization along with considerable centralized control have adopted the organizational device of special sections of the corporate industrial relations staffs assigned specifically to each division.

A comparison of the degree of centralization and decentralization in the firms studied with the presence or absence of divisional staffs does not indicate a strong relationship between them. All the firms in which there was a significant amount of decision making at the divisional level had divisional staffs. However, only 40 per cent of the firms with divisional staffs as compared with nearly 50 per cent of the companies not having such staffs have significant amounts of decision making at the plant level. The utilization of divisional staffs was found to be more closely correlated with the size of the firm as measured by total employees and number of plants.

At first thought it might seem that companies in which the industrial relations function tended toward centralization would have larger corporate staffs than those that tended more toward decentralization in this area. However, an examination of the information obtained does not bear this out. The size of the corporate staffs was compared on a basis of total company employees per staff member, excluding secretarial help on the corporate staffs.[1] Companies with centralized and those with decentralized industrial relations functions were about evenly split on either side of a median figure (for all companies reporting) of 1,000 employees per staff member. The size of corporate staffs measured in this manner is more closely related to the total number of employees in the company.

b. Organizational status of industrial relations staffs

The status of industrial relations staffs, as indicated by the title of the chief industrial relations officer and the person to whom heads of industrial relations staffs report, influence the centralization or decentralization of industrial relations in two ways. If the status of the industrial relations department is high, there may be some tendency on the part of lower levels of management to accept as authoritative directives any advice or suggestion coming from staff members. Also, if

[1] The comparison of sizes of industrial relations staffs is at best a precarious procedure since in some firms certain functions are not included under industrial relations while in other firms they are. Safety and time and motion study are two examples that come to mind immediately. Where only corporate staffs are compared, the existence of divisional staffs affect the size of the corporate staff.

the head of the industrial relations staff has a close association with top line officers, it may be possible to use the authority of superior line officers to force the acceptance of the staff's advice on recalcitrant line management at lower levels of management.

Of the 46 companies contributing information on this question, 28 give the title of director, general manager, or manager to the chief industrial relations officer. In 17 cases he is designated a vice president, and in one instance an assistant vice president. In many instances where the head of industrial relations held the rank of director or some equivalent, other heads of divisions are similarly designated rather than having the title of vice president. Consequently, in a large number of cases the industrial relations head at the corporate level is of sufficient rank to give the department status throughout the organization. A reason often given for endowing the chief industrial relations officer with such a high rank is to ensure that the top officers of the company with whom he must deal will give adequate consideration to his advice. In one sense, this in itself implies some degree of centralization of the industrial relations function.

The person to whom the head of industrial relations reports is also an indication of the status of the department in the corporation. In 37 of the 45 concerns from which information was obtained on this matter, the chief industrial relations officer reports to the president or to an executive vice president established to share some of the work load of the president. In three companies he reports to the vice president for manufacturing and, in one instance, to the vice president and general counsel.

The four remaining companies represent an interesting development in organization. In these firms the chief industrial relations officer, along with the heads of other staffs, reports to a "staff" vice president, who appears to be a variation of the military chief of staff. The use of a "staff" vice president not only removes the chief industrial relations officer one step from the president, and thus to some extent reduces his ability to utilize the authority of the president to force the acceptance of the department's advice on lower levels of line management, but it also emphasizes the advisory function of the department.

In those companies having divisional industrial relations staffs, a pattern very similar to that of the corporate level was found. In 12 of the 18 cases the head of the divisional staff reported to the top line officer of the division, either a divisional manager or a vice president. In three cases where subsidiaries, rather than divisions, were used, the chief industrial relations officer at that level reported to the president of the subsidiary. In two other instances the industrial relations department head reported to the manager of production for the division. Finally, in one company which to some extent practiced functionalized management, the head of the division staff reported to both the divisional vice president and the chief corporate industrial relations officer.

c. Composition of staff

An analysis of the basis of specialization within the corporate industrial relations staff provides some interesting comparisons with the findings in the later chapters of this report on specific industrial relations functions. As might be expected, 23 of 37 companies have sections of the corporate staff devoted to benefit plans. Although the setting of basic wage rates is often delegated to local management, 26 of the firms have sub-groups within the corporate staff for handling matters concerning wage and salary administration. This would seem to indicate management's concern with procedure that involves substantial sums of money. In addition, even though the application of policy in this area is decentralized, management wants to provide as much expert assistance as possible, and the establishment of experts at headquarters is an economical method of making such advice available. This latter factor also probably explains the large number of firms (26) having training sections in their corporate staff, even though training is perhaps the function most frequently cited as decentralized. Other aspects of the industrial relations function which were represented by sections in the corporate staff in more than half of the companies providing information on this question are employee relations and labor relations. In addition, safety and medical subdivisions were found in a majority of the companies.

One other aspect of the organization of the corporate staff which encourages centralization is the treatment of plant staffs operating in the same local area as corporate headquarters. As a hold-over from earlier days when the same staff handled both plant and corporate matters, the industrial relations department for the plants in the headquarters city in a few cases are still sections of the corporate staff. That other than historical factors may explain such arrangements is indicated by the comments of one company which stated that the work load resulting from one local plant and from corporate industrial relations matters was such that the corporate staff could take care of both. Much more widespread is a similar practice of including the industrial relations staff for the personnel working in the corporate headquarters office as part of the corporate staff.

d. Relation to staffs at lower levels

The relationship between the corporate industrial relations staff and staffs at the division or plant level provides an important avenue of centralization. The extent to which decision making occurs at a higher level as a result of that relationship depends upon the authority or influence which the corporate staff has over the other groups and the frequency of consultation between them. As indicated in Chapter IV, there is frequent contact between corporate staffs and lower levels of management.

All but one of the companies interviewed stated that the corporate staff had no direct authority over divisional or plant staffs. However, nearly 25 per cent of the firms returning the short questionnaire reported that the plant personnel manager was "primarily responsible" to the chief industrial relations executive. However, 75 per cent of the companies with such an arrangement are characterized by a small number of plants not widely distributed geographically.

From the standpoint of organizational structure, the non-authoritative type of relationship would seem to encourage decentralization more than a situation in which the corporate staff was given direct line authority over divisional and plant staffs. At least one line of direct central control is eliminated in this manner since the corporate staff supposedly could not use sanctions on lower staffs for not carrying out instructions as received from headquarters.[1]

However, in very many cases, other factors have resulted in the corporate staff having great influence on staffs at lower levels. The selection of plant industrial relations personnel and their chances of promotion depend largely upon the corporate staff. Of 19 companies reporting on this matter, ten stated that the plant manager had final authority on the employment of the plant industrial relations personnel, but that the corporate staff usually was consulted; seven that the plant manager had to have approval of the corporate staff before hiring or terminating plant staff personnel; and two, that the corporate staff hired plant personnel for such positions. Even when the ultimate authority lies with the plant manager, the advice and recommendations given by the corporate staff are likely to carry great weight. Furthermore, because of the bonds of profession and similar training, the plant industrial relations staff is likely to be more sympathetic to the ideas ot the corporate staff than to those of a line executive whenever a differ-

---

[1] Centralized control over industrial relations could, however, be maintained *via* the line organization.

ence of opinion exists. However, to the extent that the plant staff identifies itself with the plant, the countervailing pulls of the operating unit *vs.* headquarters may serve as an offsetting factor.

In very many of the cases in which the corporate staff had no direct authority over staff at lower levels, the relationship was referred to in terms of the plant staff being "functionally" responsible to the chief industrial relations executive. Some idea of what functional responsibility involves can be obtained from the following statements:

> "Plant personnel can clear problems of industrial relations directly with the chief industrial relations executive but they are expected to have discussed the matter first with the plant manager."

> ". . . the plant industrial relations manager looks to the plant manager for administrative guidance but looks to headquarters [industrial relations] for functional guidance and company-wide standards."

> "Plant personnel managers are responsible to [corporate] industrial relations executive for policy, to [plant] manager for conduct and administration."

The common thread running through all three of these statements is that the corporate industrial relations executive is the source of advice on the content and interpretation of industrial relations policies. In essence, functional responsibility would thus seem to mean only that a direct line of communication is available between the corporate staff and plant staffs on matters concerning industrial relations policies and procedures. As indicated above, no line authority is involved in most relationships between plant and corporate staffs and therefore no responsibility in a strict organizational sense can exist between them. However, the indirect influences discussed previously may informally achieve that result.

B. Plant Organization

1. *Line management*

a. Levels of supervision and span of control

The general organization of a plant like that of the corporation is a factor in the degree of centralization or decentralization of the industrial relations function. Information on plant organization was obtained largely from the nine plants in which extensive interviewing was done as part of the four case studies made. A substantial amount of information was obtained also from nine other factories in the group of companies that were primarily interviewed at corporate headquarters. Three of the case-study companies, comprising seven plants, represented highly mechanized process type of industries. Most of the plants were of medium size, only two employing over 1,300 workers. The two large plants had 5,000 and 3,000 employees respectively.

Despite the modest size of the plants, substantial hierarchies of supervision were found in many of them. Six levels of supervision was the most common for plants over 500 employees. The number of levels reported ranged from three to seven, with only one plant reporting each of these extremes. One of the results of having many levels of supervision in plants of the size studied was a small span of control, particularly below the two top levels: plant manager and divisional superintendents. Almost all of the former had seven or more subordinates reporting to them. The same was true for only about half of the superintendents. However, supervisors at the department head and general foreman level very frequently had only two or three members of lower levels of management reporting to them. One important factor explaining such an organizational structure is the complicated manufacturing processes of the companies studied and the need, therefore, of technically trained supervisors. Although that group concentrates on the operation of equipment, it is still necessary that they have line authority over other levels of supervision.

The combination of small span of control and many levels of management makes it feasible for lower levels of supervision to refer industrial relations matters to their superiors. With such small numbers involved at any one level, personal contact between the first line of supervision and the second and third strata is frequent and easy. In some cases, the first three or four levels of management occupy the same office.

The span of control of the first line of supervision, also, is important to centralization and decentralization. If first line supervisors are to carry out the industrial relations policies of the company, they must have time not only to spend on the specific personnel problems as they arise but also to learn about human relations, new industrial relations policies, and changes in union contracts. Consequently, foremen cannot be assigned so many men or technical duties as to prohibit satisfactory performance in this area.

It is impossible to determine even an approximate normal range for the span of control of a first line supervisor. Figures encountered in the plants interviewed ran from five to eighty, although in the latter case there was an admitted policy of spreading supervision thin. The nature of the production process, the type of worker, and the state of employee and union relations, in addition to the ability of the foreman, all affect the number of men assigned to each supervisor. It is worthy of note that decentralization of decision making need not be confined to management. Responsibilities for decisions concerning production can be, and in some cases studied were, given to rank-and-file employees, particularly in the case of skilled operators.

b. Basis of subdivision

As indicated in the discussion of organizational structure at the corporate level, it has been argued that decentralization of general management is feasible only if the organization is divided into sub-units which encompass the important elements of the operation. At the plant and intra-plant levels of organization, considerations of cost often work against division into integrated sub-units. The degree of integration found varied considerably. However, in none of the case-study companies were plant managers responsible for sales as well as production and in most cases the most important raw materials were centrally purchased.

c. Shift supervision

Although it is not often considered in discussions of organization, the arrangement of supervisors where shifts are rotated is often of importance to the degree of centralization. Under one plan, only a few members of management are in charge of the afternoon and night shifts, and regular foremen work the day shift only. The latter then are responsible for industrial relations matters for all employees working in their sections regardless of the shift. In another arrangement, a foreman is assigned to each group of workers on a shift schedule and rotates with the workers. In both of these types of organization the foreman can still deal with the industrial relations problems of the employees.

However, a third manner of organizing shift work tends to move decisions to a higher level. Foremen are assigned to each shift but do not rotate at the same time that workers do. Thus, in any given week there is likely to be a different combination of foremen and workers than the previous. Because of this lack of continuity of foreman-worker relationship there is some risk that none of the foremen will accept responsibility for the industrial relations problems of workers. Furthermore, even slight differences in application of policies or contracts in such a situation will be evident, thus tending to place responsibility for the decision on a common higher supervisor.

2. *Plant industrial relations staffs*

The size of the industrial relations staff in plants studied ranged up to 30. One plant of about 40 employees had no staff at all and another of approximately 300 employees had one individual who spent half his time on industrial relations and half on purchases. Forty per cent of the plants had between six and ten employees on the industrial relations staff. The remaining plants were split equally between those having more than ten and those having less than six.

The size of staffs was largely determined by the size of the plants. As one company put it, "plant staffs vary from 2 in one of the small plants to 22 in a large plant, where employment is 2700." No attempt was made to correlate the ratio of employees to staff members with the tendency toward centralization or decentralization within the company because too little information was available.

Some specialization of function occurred within plant staffs of more than two or three members. Employment, medical and safety specialists were found in almost all cases. The organizational chart for plant staffs showed a separate training section in about half the cases. Benefits and wage and salary groups were reported in about one-quarter of the cases. It should be pointed out that the absence of specifically designated sections for various industrial relations activities does not indicate that plant staffs do not provide services in such areas. The relatively small size of most plant staffs preclude having specialists in all areas.

In all of the plants studied, the head of the industrial relations staff reported to the plant manager and in most cases was given a title similar to that of plant division heads. In addition, with a few exceptions, the head of industrial relations was a member of the top committee in the plant for decision making on plant problems. Added together, these gave the industrial relations staff considerable status in the plant. Thus their advice took on additional aspects of authority.

C. EFFECTS OF ORGANIZATIONAL STRUCTURE ON THE LEVEL OF DECISION MAKING

The foregoing analysis has indicated a number of ways in which the organizational structure may affect the level of decision making. One of the more important ways in which this occurs is indirectly as the structure emphasizes the peculiar nature of a subdivision of the corporation, either as a result of organization along product lines or from maintaining the separate corporate identity of merged subsidiaries, and thereby encourages decision making at the divisional level. In addition, the structure of organization may contribute to a reduction of the flow of communications and thus informally permit greater decision making at lower levels purely because higher levels are not aware of the problem requiring a decision.

Perhaps the most important aspect of the organizational structure affecting the level of decision making on industrial relations matters is the creation of staffs of experts at high levels in the management hierarchy in both the corporation and plant. Line management is more likely to refer decisions on industrial relations matters to such specialists than to superiors in the line who are no more qualified than themselves in this area. Decision making becomes more centralized as a result, unless the staff confines its role completely to giving advice. The fact that the staffs are experts, however, may mean that their advice is accepted as a final decision. In addition the organizational status of the industrial relations staff may contribute to the acceptance of their advice as authoritative directives.

The close relationship of the corporate staff to plant staffs also increases the degree of possible centralization as a result of referrals by line management to the industrial relations staffs. Although the formal organizational structure does not give the central staff direct authority over plant staffs, the informal relationships of these two groups results in the corporate staff having great influence over staffs at lower levels.

As the following chapters will indicate, the duties assigned to the industrial relations staff create additional opportunities for indirect decision making by this group. Further, the discussion below of the responsibility for decisions on specific functions will indicate that in some cases line authority for decisions on industrial relations matters has been directly assigned to the industrial relations staffs. As a result, decision making becomes more centralized.

GENERAL RESPONSIBILITY FOR THE
INDUSTRIAL RELATIONS FUNCTION

IV. LOCATION OF GENERAL RESPONSIBILITY FOR THE INDUSTRIAL RELATIONS FUNCTION

AS stated in Chapter I, for the purpose of this study we have divided the broad concept of administrative decision making for industrial relations into three parts: policy, implementation of policy, and application of policy. This chapter describes today's general practice in these three aspects of decision making for industrial relations. It also attempts to compare *general practice* with the determination, implementation, and application of *specific* industrial relations policies,[1] and to compare current practice with common practice in 1937 and 1947.

A. CURRENT GENERAL PRACTICE

With rare exceptions, the companies studied expressed a strong philosophy of line responsibility for industrial relations. This responsibility was seen as extending from the top level of management down to and including the first line supervisor. The findings indicate that this philosophy is put into effect to the extent that policy decisions are accepted as the responsibility of a chief executive or group of executives and as the application of policy is accepted as the responsibility of lower levels of operating management. The 88 companies answering a question as to the basis on which major industrial relations policies are established replied as follows:

On a company-wide basis	72
By each plant	2
Varies	14

The 84 companies in this group giving information as to the management level in which responsibility for the application of policies was centered, replied:

At headquarters	26
At the plant	58

The criteria of a major policy remain the same as in previous studies. Stated in terms relevant to centralization and decentralization, they are: (1) the subject is a matter that affects the corporation as a whole

[1] See Chapters VI-IX.

or at least more than the one unit in which the question for decision is first raised; (2) the amount of money involved is greater than the individual plant or the unit of organization first concerned is generally permitted to spend without approval; and (3) the policy relates to the area of bargaining or other union-management matters affecting particularly the balance of bargaining power. Conversely, less important industrial relations policies that may be determined at a plant or division level are those affecting only the one unit of the corporation, are within the financial limits permitted the unit, and are not an issue in union-management relations that may challenge management's bargaining strength. However, even in matters meeting all of these criteria for policy decisions that can be delegated, few policies were found to be established by a plant manager without consultation with the division or headquarters' staff.

As indicated by the answer of 14 companies, "sometimes one and sometimes the other," the level of decision making is affected by changing circumstances. The variable factors in the level of policy making are revealed most clearly in connection with specific policies.[1] However, as a number of companies with an organizational distinction between personnel administration and labor relations commented, more leeway is generally allowed plant management in activities included in personnel administration than in those in the labor relations category.

1. *The development and determination of policy*

The responsibility of top management for the industrial relations function is shown most clearly in procedures in the final determination of major industrial relations policies. Such determination is seldom a matter of individual decision. Of the 46 companies interviewed, 34 reported that final decisions on industrial relations policies were made by an executive committee, management council, or board of directors. In ten companies, final decision was made on a less formal basis by the president, an executive vice president, or by the industrial relations manager in consultation with one or more top executives. In only two of the 46 companies were industrial relations policies made principally at a subsidiary level. In one of these, the officers of the parent corporation are members of subsidiary boards, insuring adequate consideration of the corporation point of view. In the other, there is frequent informal consultation between the corporation and subsidiary boards and between industrial relations staffs of subsidiaries and the corporation.

The industrial relations staff enters directly into the process of mak-

[1] See Chapters VI to IX.

ing policy decisions not only through informal discussions with a chief executive, but also through membership on a committee or council that makes final decision. Of the 34 companies in which industrial relations policies are determined by a committee, council, or board, nine stated that the corporation director of industrial relations was a member of the decision-making body. Responsibility for the initiation of a policy change rests primarily with the corporation industrial relations staff. Suggestions for change are often made by plant line supervisors and executives and sometimes come up through the line organization. However, most of the industrial relations people interviewed considered it an important part of their job to be alert to changes within or outside the company that indicated the need for policy change. Moreover, the principal line of communicating suggestions upward was evidently through the plant staff to the headquarters staff. It appeared also that suggestions that resulted in study by the staff and discussion looking towards a recommendation of new policy came as frequently from top management as from lower levels.

The formulation of policy statements is also primarily a function of the headquarters industrial relations staff. Only 12 of the 46 companies reported the existence of one or more high level management committees responsible in whole or in part for the formulation of industrial relations policies. In at least half of these companies, the committees dealt only with limited subject areas, such as benefits, salaries, or executive development. The following company statements illustrate the principal types of procedure in policy formulation and determination. They also reveal the almost inevitable variations in practice that affect the degree of centralization or decentralization.

"Theoretically the Board of Directors has final authority for all principal policies of the company including important industrial relations policies. It also has final authority on certain matters that are not policy changes such as a general wage change or any modification or improvement in a benefit program. In practice, however, decision is made by the management committee. The management committee is made up of the president, the vice president of operations, the vice presidents of production, personnel, marketing, research engineering, the general counsel, and the treasurer. This committee actually has no explicit authority for decision making, but the Board almost invariably accepts its recommendations."

"The senior management committee of the company is the Operating Committee. This group consists of all officers of the company and general managers of all departments. In the field of industrial relations is the Industrial and Public Relations Committee. Usually all major departments are represented on this committee. The Operating Committee, as the major group, can overrule the actions of the Industrial and Public Relations Committee, but in practice the duplication of personnel enables the two groups to arrive at a common policy. The latter committee is limited to the extent that it cannot approve the expenditure of money. In some instances, a very small group may actually make the decision. Because of the necessity for secrecy in such matters as company ceiling on wage allowances, the [head of industrial relations] and two or three others would make the decision."

"There is no formal procedure for the formulation of and final decision on changes in principal industrial relations policies, etc. The Vice President and Director of Industrial Relations and Vice President and Operating Manager discuss, decide, and where they deem it advisable discuss the particular question further with other interested top executives."

The chief industrial relations officer making the last statement also commented in a later interview that in his opinion an operating man should *not* control industrial relations decisions.

The response of one of the two corporations reporting that industrial relations policies are determined by the subsidiary companies shows the complicated structure of decision making, the extensive discussion that precedes a decision on policy, and the catalytic role played by the industrial relations staff in arriving at a decision satisfactory to affiliates and parent corporation.

The Employee Relations managers of the principal affiliates meet twice a year under the sponsorship of the Employee Relations Department of the parent company. The meeting generally concerns itself with problems and projects affecting the long-run picture, but some problems of current interest are taken up, particularly those affecting wages and other labor relations. The group can make recommendations to their respective principals and frequently do. In this manner coordination and some uniformity result without weakening the major policy of decentralization.

The parent company's Employee Relations Department Advisory Committee is made up of the top echelon of the department. It functions as an advisory group on current problems, assists the manager in overall planning of work of the department, and serves as a communication medium. By having a rotating attendance from one member of the lower echelon, it provides an opportunity for orientation and training for overall employee relations operations and thinking.

Individual plant managers or heads of affiliates are encouraged to handle their own employee relations problems at the plant or affiliate level in every possible case. Thus, the employee relations manager at the plant or affiliate must be a person selected for his ability to understand the possible complications which could arise when the plant or affiliate takes an action which might affect [the company as a whole]. If he feels that his superior . . . is about to take such an action, he advises him not to do so without first seeking information from central headquarters of his own company or the parent company.

2. *The implementation of policy*

The same materials and the same type of person-to-person discussion that implements policy may also be coordinative media and, as such, they are discussed at length in Chapter V. It is necessary, however, to consider implementation as a step between the determination and the application of policy since it is a means of relating policy more directly to its application and thus limits the discretion of those responsible for its application to specific situations. Whatever the form, implementation specifies in detail how a given plan or policy is to be handled by the various levels of management. The area of implementation may be observed most easily in the difference between policy statements in a handbook for employees and in the statement of policy and procedure in a supervisors' manual.

The forging of the implementing procedures, other than those worked out in negotiations with the union, is largely the responsibility of the head industrial relations staff. While special high level committees that formulate and recommend industrial relations policies may also assist in the preparation of manuals of procedure, such committees are more likely to approve what has been done by the industrial relations staff than actively participate in the preparation of the manual, letter, or statement of procedure. The job specification for one manager of industrial relations differentiated as follows between the development of policy on the one hand and of procedures on the other:

"Duties and Responsibilities. . . .

2. To develop and recommend industrial relations policies which will provide the means of obtaining, maintaining and dealing with an efficient and cooperative employee group. . . .

5. To supervise the development of procedures and methods for installing and maintaining program projects at all applicable locations. To review and approve procedures and plans developed within the department, and to assist in their execution. . . ."

Less formalized responsibility for implementation was indicated in such comments as this:

Policy questions are hammered out by the department manager and in executive conference. Once the policy has been decided upon, letters in regard to it are prepared by the central industrial relations office and then given to the operating heads for their signature and to send out. The central industrial relations staff exerts an influence both through conference with the directors and by writing the letters announcing policy and suggesting or prescribing procedures. However, whatever the central industrial relations staff does is always subject to criticism or final decision either by the executive conference, in case of policies, or by the department heads, in case of interpretation and procedures. . . .

Informal oral interpretation by the plant and central industrial relations staffs was reported by many companies. Sometimes such informal interpretation not only makes a given policy more explicit, but extends upward into policy making and downward into application. As the scope of labor agreements expands, implementing procedures as well as policies become more frequently subject to negotiation. The developments in a number of companies suggest that the increase in informal consultation may be at least partly the result of the increase in the items subject to negotiations. Their experience also suggests that informal interpretation may be adopted as a means of facilitating the acceptance of centralized decision making.

3. *Application of policy*

Without exception corporate management and top plant management of the companies in which plant managers were interviewed stated their belief that decisions on the application of industrial relations policies should be made as far down the line as possible. As far as could be determined from information from various levels of management, application of policy is the responsibility of plant management *with exceptions and within limitations*. The exceptions commonly include such matters as wage and salary changes, interpretation of labor agreements, leaves of absence, and early or postponed retirement under a compulsory plan. The limitations include prescribed procedures (discussed under implementation), customary or required consultation prior to decision, and required headquarters approval of agreements negotiated locally.

The depth of delegation of application involving discretionary judgment is rarely below that of the general foreman. First line foremen rarely have the authority to take final action without consultation. Moreover, higher levels that have such authority are likely to consult with the plant industrial relations manager before making a decision.[1]

---

[1] This question is discussed in more detail in Chapters IX and X.

The difference should be pointed out between application of policies permitting some variation in decision on the one hand, and the transmittal of decisions or other supervisor-employee contacts not involving decision making on the other. Companies emphasizing their belief that "the administration of industrial relations policies must be decentralized to the point of contact between employees and the first line supervision" appear to be referring to *methods* and *personal relationships rather than* to the *delegation of discretion in decision making.*

B. The Role of the Industrial Relations Staffs

The heads of corporate industrial relations staffs consider their roles as having five principal aspects. These are: (1) to counsel and make specific recommendations to those responsible for policy decisions; (2) to carry on research relative to the need and formulation of policy; (3) to prepare interpretations of policies and procedures to be followed by the line in applying policy (implementation) and to assist the line in its responsibility for the application of policies; (4) to serve as a two-way channel of information both in developing policies and facilitating their uniform interpretation and application; and (5) to make decisions or to participate in decision making as a member of a policy-making group or as agent of management in the application of policies.

Heads of industrial relations staffs are in agreement on the first four aspects of the job. Most of them also think it desirable to be a member of a policy-making group. They favor this not in order to be a dominating figure in policy decisions but to be certain that the industrial relations point of view is given adequate consideration and to have an opportunity to get the consensus of opinion of operating executives. The greatest division of opinion concerning the role of the industrial relations staff is in the area of direct decision making. On this point, opinion seemed to depend on the situation in which the head of industrial relations found himself. If he was in a position where he often had to make decisions, he felt that this was necessary and proper; if he was acting wholly in an informational, advisory, and implementary role, he felt that any greater authority was undesirable. The men in less clearly defined positions were aware of the problems involved in decision making by staff but also recognized how easy it was to slip into a position in which advice was accepted as decision.

In reporting to the plant manager, the plant industrial relations manager duplicates in his smaller sphere the role of the corporation industrial relations manager: that is, he advises and informs the plant manager but also, as his agent, often handles certain industrial relations activities and makes day-to-day decisions. He also advises lower levels of management. In his functional responsibility to the industrial relations manager he is, in a sense, an extension of the headquarters staff into the plant. In this role, he serves as a two-way channel of information. Also, insofar as the headquarters staff makes decisions, the plant industrial relations manager may be called upon to carry out the decision or to make sure that it is carried out in his plant.

No specific question was asked of company presidents as to their opinion of the function of industrial relations staffs. However, comment was often volunteered on this point. All direct definition of function emphasized the informational and advisory nature of the industrial relations staff. Other statements implied that members of the central industrial relations staff were a part of the framework limiting plant autonomy. One company, for example, whose present goal is as complete decentralization as possible stated:

> "Because we want our employment relationships at all of our subsidiary locations to be *uniformly* good we, of course, have an overall philosophy and specific policies to guide our general managers. However, the actions of the local managers, *within the broad limitations of established principle and policy and with the advice and counsel of our Central Staff Service Personnel Department*,[1] are not directed from headquarters."

A company president, emphasizing the need for balance between centralization and decentralization, lumped the plant managers and industrial relations managers together in reference to application of policies:

> "Sometimes it is difficult to know just where to draw the line but I believe that it works out best . . . to lay down some broad general principles and then give plant managers and industrial relations managers considerable latitude within the scope of those general principles."

Whatever the formal definition of the role of the industrial relations staff, it is evident that the headquarters staff in a majority of companies studied plays a role in the determination of policy only second to that of top management. As an agent of top management, it is a centralizing influence. The plant industrial relations staff representing, in turn, an extension of the headquarters staff into the plant is also a factor in centralization. As a member of the staff of the plant executive, the local industrial relations manager also presents the local point of view to headquarters. In the latter respect he is facilitating decentralization.

[1] Italics added.

Which part of his job is given the greater emphasis is one measure of the balance of centralization and decentralization.

C. Extent and Form of Participation

1. *The background of participation*

In spite of the limitations on the discretion of line executives below the top level, those who were interviewed from division or plant management were almost invariably of the opinion that they had full responsibility for maintaining sound industrial relations in their jurisdictions. Nor were there any indications that these executives felt they had more responsibility than authority.

A number of things may account for this attitude in the face of their limited area of discretion. One of these, as referred to above, is the acceptance of industrial relations as a matter of *personal relationships* rather than one of *decision making*. Another is the common assumption that a high degree of uniformity is necessary and that a common body of knowledge is basic to this. A third is the feeling throughout all levels of management today that industrial relations problems—in broad or narrow terms—cannot be solved by one person. The possible repercussions from a single misjudgment may be unexpectedly troublesome. The lower ranks of supervision are content to avoid responsibility for any but the most minor decisions, and higher plant management is quite willing to clear (or have the plant industrial relations manager clear) with headquarters. All ranks of management expect to consult with other levels before making a decision. They also expect to be consulted, especially on matters on which they are best informed and most competent. They are resentful of decisions that affect them and that have been made without consideration of their particular problems.

2. *The nature and methods of participation*

Participation is a term used to describe activities that range from a vice president's contribution to a decision as a member of a top management committee to a casual conversation between the plant industrial relations manager and a foreman. As plant managers and supervisors see it, participation involves the right and opportunity to make suggestions and to criticize, the expectation of being consulted prior to action affecting their specific jurisdictions, and, at least, representation in decisions if they are to be held responsible for results.

The following methods of participation were reported by corporation industrial relations staffs and plant personnel.

a. An actual sharing in the decision-making process

In the determination of company-wide industrial relations policies this formal sharing in decision making rarely goes below the heads of divisions or key plants. Informally, the majority of cooperating companies attempt to secure and evaluate plant management opinions before making decisions that will affect them. When the plant manager or a supervisor is nominally responsible for the decision, the referral upward may be voluntary informal discussion or may be required approval by a higher level. Just as a policy decision may be the result of group discussion, so decision on application of policy at the plant may be made by a formal grievance committee or in an informal exchange of views to arrive at a common understanding of what should be done.

b. Formal solicitation of suggestions and criticism from the plant-line and staff

Formal procedure was reported most frequently with reference to the development of a printed statement of industrial relations policies or with reference to discussion prior to negotiation of the labor agreement. The headquarters and plant industrial relations staffs are generally responsible for seeing that this formal consultation is carried on, although the head of the division or plant may sign letters of request or be in charge of group meetings in which ideas and criticisms are solicited.

c. Informal noting and reporting of line opinion

This informal, person-to-person discussion was considered important not only in getting ideas, but in gaining impressions and giving a sense of participation. The key role played by the industrial relations staff, especially in informal procedures, was suggested by such comments as the following:

> The principal means of getting the plant executives' and supervisors' points of view [on industrial relations] is through division and plant industrial relations managers who are expected to keep in touch with executive and supervisory opinion.

> We need better plant personnel men to facilitate plant participation.

> The field industrial relations men are of great help in getting the opinion of line people.

Regular plant management meetings at several levels were also mentioned as channels for foremen comment to upper levels and were reported as the most important channel in a few companies. For example, one of the most decentralized companies reported:

"No company-wide pattern [of participation] but in most cases the vice president has a committee made up of plant managers and other key people with whom changes in policy are discussed. The central industrial relations staff is ordinarily not in on such consultation except to supply information."

3. *The extent and evaluation of participation*

a. Extent

Eighty-nine companies responded to the question, "To what extent do plant executives participate in the development of company-wide policies?" Fifty-seven replied "extensively on most policies"; 18, "extensively on a few policies"; 8, "casually on most policies"; and 6, "plant management rarely consulted."

A closer look at participation in the 46 companies interviewed gave a somewhat different impression. All of them reported some participation by plant management in the development of company-wide industrial relations policies. Twenty-nine companies referred to one or more formal as well as a variety of informal procedures used to a varying extent according to the subject and the urgency of the situation. Nine mentioned only the wide use of informal methods; and the representatives of eight companies reported that any downward consultation was infrequent and, in their opinion, inadequate. Of these eight, four felt that too little thought had been given to plant management participation in centrally determined policies because it was still assumed that many policies were determined locally.

Outstanding impressions of the extent and form of participation gained from the interviews were: (1) participation was as often directed by and through staff as through line channels; (2) companies are increasingly interested in getting plant participation and only a small minority of the reporting companies failed to express such an interest; and (3) participation is informal and varies in extent according to subject more frequently than it is formal and consistently extensive.

b. Evaluation

The value of participation is almost wholly a matter of opinion. Moreover opinions varied greatly as to what is sought and what may be gained. The gains on which there is general agreement are the educational value (improved understanding of management's aims and problems), and the sense of sharing in a common responsibility. Some believed the ideas secured through participation of plant managers and supervisors were important contributions to the vitality of the organization; others felt they were not. Many commented especially on the paucity of useful ideas from supervisors.

The following quotations reflect the opinions of corporation industrial relations executives with respect to the participation of lower levels of management in industrial relations matters on which decisions are made at a higher level:

"Principal problems [of decentralization] are the time involved in securing participation, interest, and approval by operating executives and plant management. . . . In our Company, the Vice President of Operations and plant managers hold monthly operating meetings. We are given a good opportunity to present industrial relations problems and programs at that meeting—to follow up with managers later—and to secure decisions. No major industrial relations or public relations program is instituted unless the Assistant to the President—Industrial and Public Relations *and* Vice President of Operations are in agreement and are certain that local works management understands the program thoroughly and the effort, money, and participation involved. This approach results (1) in slower, but more consistent, progress; (2) in more realistic programs; (3) in more participation by all echelons of works management . . . ; (4) in more freedom of criticism by all concerned; (5) in fewer fads . . . ; (6) in readiness to measure value of programs."

— —   — —   — —

Participation often brings out enough additional information to modify predetermined cases. It is much more than giving a psychological sense of participation. It is really getting the best judgment of a whole group.

— —   — —   — —

The upward flow of information is not perfect but over the years we have convinced the members of supervision that they can make suggestions, and supervisors feel that they have some influence. . . .

— —   — —   — —

When the company has sought plant opinion, top management has received some good ideas. But, of more importance, consultation has increased goodwill throughout plant management.

— —   — —   — —

Plant management is usually consulted but lower levels of supervision are very seldom brought into the discussion. For one reason, the issues are too technical for foremen to make any suggestions, and for another, we don't want any leaks to employees until a policy is definite.

D. Trend in Location of Responsibility for the Industrial Relations Function

The appraisal of a general trend, even based to as large an extent as possible on reported statements of practice, is primarily an accumulation of impressions. The evidence consists of conflicting opinions, variable practices, and descriptions of the industrial relations staff job that do not always agree with what the people on the job report they are doing. Nevertheless the effort has been made to compare reports from similar groups of companies (sometimes the same companies) over a period of time, and also to compare the opinion as to general trend with reported changes in practice in specific industrial relations activities.

1. *Company opinion as to change*

The industrial relations executives interviewed in 46 companies were asked their opinion concerning the trend towards centralization or decentralization of the industrial relations function in their own companies in the past ten years. The results are shown in Table 4.

TABLE 4. OPINION AS TO CHANGE IN THE DEGREE
OF CENTRALIZATION AND DECENTRALIZATION IN PAST TEN YEARS

Trend	No. of companies
Definitely towards centralization	5
Mixed, but inclined towards centralization	8
Definitely towards decentralization	6
Mixed, but inclined towards decentralization	20
Little change (generally centralized)	2
Little change (company is felt to have optimum decentralization)	5

It is clear that the majority of company executives interviewed felt that the trend has been toward decentralization. While 60 per cent (28 companies) see that some activities have become more centralized as others have become less so, the opinions concerning definite or mixed trends or no change, taken as a whole, show that the executives interviewed believe decentralization has gained in the past ten years.

2. *Comparison of information received in 1938, 1947, and 1953*

Thirteen companies (28 per cent of the concerns in the current study) cooperated in two previous studies of the Industrial Relations Section concerning the determination of industrial relations policies. Information received from these companies in 1938,[1] 1947,[1] and 1952-53 was studied for evidence of trends in each one. Comparison was made between the conclusions of trend drawn from the two earlier studies and from practices reported in the present study and these conclusions compared with company opinion recently expressed as to their trend in the last ten years. The results of these comparisons are shown in Table 5.

TABLE 5. TREND IN THIRTEEN COMPANIES AS CONCLUDED FROM
PRACTICE REPORTED IN THREE STUDIES COMPARED
WITH COMPANY OPINION AS TO RECENT TREND

Conclusions as to trend resulting from review of information received in 1938, 1947 and 1953	No. of cos.	Recent company opinion of trend 1943-1953 in same companies	No. of cos.
Moved from decentralization to greater centralization and back toward decentralization	2	Mixed but inclined to more centralization Mixed but inclined to more decentralization	1 1
Fluctuating and variable movement—inclining especially towards more centralization in labor relations	8	Mixed but inclined toward decentralization Little change—steady decentralization	6 2
Moved steadily towards greater centralization	3	Definitely towards centralization	3

Table 5 suggests two conclusions: (1) The movement between centralization and decentralization of the industrial relations function is more often variable than clearly and steadily one way or the other. This supports the belief of a majority of industrial relations executives reported in Chapter II that the balance between the two must vary according to circumstance. (2) Management opinion received in 1952 and 1953 tended to overemphasize the trend towards decentralization.

The trend since 1938 was also examined on the basis of information received from the groups of companies as a whole at the three different periods.[2] The particular subjects on which there was comparable information were: (1) the location of general responsibility for the determination of industrial relations policies; (2) procedures in the

[1] See Baker, H. *The Determination and Administration of Industrial Relations Policies.* Princeton University, Industrial Relations Section. 1939; and *Management Procedures in the Determination of Industrial Relations Policies.* 1948.

[2] The 1938 survey included 100 companies of which 58 were multiplant; the 1947 survey covered 84 companies of which 73 were multiplant; the 1952-53 survey included 46 companies all of which were multiplant, plus 89 companies replying to the short questionnaire.

formulation and determination of policies; and (3) the status of chief industrial relations executives.

a. Location of general responsibility for the determination of industrial relations policies

Study of the information received on this point in 1938, 1947, and 1952-53 revealed the greatest contrast between 1938 and 1947. The desire for greater centralization and greater uniformity in personnel policies stated frequently in 1938[1] and further accentuated by wartime controls and other factors resulted in a strong movement towards centralization. By 1947, 59 out of 73 multiplant companies reported that decisions on major industrial relations policies for the company as a whole were made "by or near top management." It was concluded in regard to the remaining 14 companies that "complete decentralization . . . exists only in the areas in which top management has not recommended policies for general adoption."[2] The location of responsibility for policy decisions appears to have moved slightly towards centralization since 1947 in spite of the increasing interest in decentralization. In the 1947 study, 19 per cent (14) of the cooperating multiplant companies reported a considerable number of personnel policies determined at plant level as compared with slightly over two per cent of the 89 companies replying to the short questionnaire in 1953 and slightly under nine per cent of the 46 companies interviewed in 1952-53.

b. Procedures in the formulation and determination of policies

A problem worrying many industrial relations executives in 1938 was the lack of definite procedures to insure clear and well considered policies. It was stated in the 1939 report that policies often "have grown up without any definite and authoritative formulation by a responsible executive or executive committee."[3] The 1947 findings indicated that procedures in the formulation of industrial relations policies were considerably more formalized: the headquarters industrial relations department had been given primary responsibility for "getting a policy into written form" in many companies, and, in a few, special high level committees had been set up to formulate policy changes.

The 1953 findings show a continuing increase in the use of com-

---

[1] *Determination and Administration of Industrial Relations Policies.* Especially p. 19.
[2] *Management Procedures in the Determination of Industrial Relations Policies,* pp. 64-65.
[3] *Determination and Administration of Industrial Relations Policies,* p. 9.

mittees, councils, and boards in the determination of policy. Thirty-nine (53 per cent) of the 73 multiplant companies in the 1947 study referred to a committee, council, or board as being principally responsible for decision on major industrial relations policies. A greater proportion (74 per cent) of the 46 companies interviewed for the current study reported that one or another such group was principally responsible. This increase in group decision making as compared with decisions made by one or a few executives is considered a move towards decentralization since such an arrangement is usually made to assure all the principal divisions of a company representation in the group decision. However, the committees or boards rarely include executives below the second level of the hierarchy. The extent to which plant management has an opportunity to offer suggestions in policy development or is permitted to use its discretion in the application of policy is not necessarily affected.

In all of the three studies, it has appeared that, to the extent that policies are established on a company-wide basis, the headquarters industrial relations staff has played a more important role than plant management in policy development. The influence which the staff has exerted, however, either through recommendation or through membership in a policy-making group has depended to some extent on its status in the organization.

c. Status of industrial relations staff

The upward movement in the status of the chief industrial relations officer that appeared between 1938 and 1947 seems to have slowed down by 1953. The 1947 survey found that 27 per cent of the companies studied reported a higher title or other indication of upward change in the status of the individual heading the industrial relations staff. No specific question concerning change in title was asked in 1952-53. However, information concerning the title of the head of industrial relations and the title of the officer to whom he reported is available for 1938, 1947, and 1953 for the thirteen companies cooperating in all three studies. These companies showed the following movement in title of the industrial relations executive between 1938 and 1947: no change, 7; higher title, 6. The record as between 1947 and 1953 was: no change, 9; higher title, 2; lower title, 2. The record of change between 1938 and 1947 with respect to the officer *to whom the industrial relations head reported* is as follows: no change, 8; a higher executive, 4; a lower executive, 1. For the 1947-1953 period the record is: no change, 7; a higher executive, 2; a lower executive, 4. The difference between recent changes in title, on the one hand, and in the rank of the individual reported to, on the other, is accounted for in part by reorganizations in three companies in which an executive vice president or a vice president of staffs had been appointed to reduce the number of people reporting directly to the president.

Changes in such a small number of companies is in itself of little significance. Nevertheless it is worth noting that the change between 1938 and 1947 in almost half of the 13 companies to a higher title for the head of industrial relations coincides with other indications of a marked increase in centralization during that period; and that the slight change between 1947 and 1953 towards reporting to a vice president instead of the president coincides with an increase in corporate reorganization setting up vice presidents of staff or delegating greater responsibility to divisional management.

3. Comparison of present opinion as to general trend with information concerning trend in specific industrial relations functions

The difficulties in attempting to estimate the movement towards more or less decentralization of a specific activity are similar to the problems in weighing the trend for the industrial relations function in general. These difficulties, however, are reduced in proportion to the size of the specific function being considered. It is, for example, difficult to see any distinct trend towards more centralization or more decentralization in the employment function as a whole; but, if broken down into employment for rank and file, for college recruiting, and for technicians and professional people, the movement for each is clearer. Such a break-down of specific functions is given in detail in Chapters VI to IX. The summary of those detailed changes is referred to here only to compare with company opinion as to general trend.

Of the 21 specific industrial relations activities analyzed with respect to the level at which policy is determined, implemented, and applied, 9 have continued to be handled at about the same levels, 9 are referred to or handled at a higher level, and only 3 have more distinct elements of decentralization than previously. Thus while divergent tendencies are apparent when the general industrial relations function is divided into specific activities, the analysis indicates a stronger movement towards centralization than decentralization, in contrast to the opinion of company executives.

V. COORDINATION AND CONTROL

COORDINATION and control are necessary under either centralized or decentralized industrial relations programs. Decision making must be delegated on at least some aspects of the application of policy in even the most centralized multiplant firms. At the other extreme, the possible impact on one plant of decisions made in another requires some coordination in a firm whose branches are otherwise permitted autonomy in establishing and carrying out industrial relations policies.

The need for coordination and control has been intensified in recent years by the spread of unionization, increased speed of communications, and increased government regulation. In meeting the need for coordination, management has relied upon various means of communication but has placed its greatest reliance upon informal methods with particular emphasis on personal contacts and consultation with higher levels of authority. Control procedures have not been developed as thoroughly as methods of coordination, and control has tended more towards checking to see that centrally determined policies are carried out than towards an audit of the overall condition of industrial relations in the plants.

The biggest obstacle to the coordination of industrial relations matters has been unsatisfactory communication. In addition, diverse local conditions, particularly varying union situations, and the inability of local personnel to see the implications of their action on other plants have increased the difficulty of obtaining uniform application of policy. In some cases, the unwillingness of local units to accept wholeheartedly centrally determined policies has prevented proper coordination.

Coordination and control result in most cases in a greater degree of centralization. To a certain extent the very nature of the processes involves limitations on the decision-making powers of local units. In addition, the emphasis on personal contacts and consultation on specific cases provides numerous opportunities for the corporate staff to exercise marked influence on the local application of policy.

A. Factors Emphasizing Need for Coordination and Control

1. *Spread of unionization*

The importance of coordination and control of the industrial relations activities in a firm has been enhanced by the spread of unionization.

The central theme in those parts of the interviews and replies to questionnaires dealing with these matters was the problem of avoiding seemingly innocuous action in one plant which the union could use to the disadvantage of the company in obtaining similar treatment at another site. That problem is greatest in companies where the various contracting local unions are all members of the same national union. However, even when independent unions or locals of different national organizations are involved, their willingness to cooperate at least to the extent of exchanging information results in only a less acute need for coordination and control within the company.

2. *Need for uniformity and fairness*

To a very large extent many of the management group interviewed believed that employees felt that, since they were working for the same corporation, fairness required uniform treatment regardless of the location. Even in the absence of a union, news of industrial relations matters spreads throughout the firm rapidly. In one instance studied, the transmission of such information was facilitated by the transfer of workers and lower levels of supervision from one plant to a newly established factory and by the personal contacts that employees in one site had with friends and relatives at other locations.

3. *Other factors*

Management also is encouraged to establish some sort of a coordinating system so that information on successful techniques developed in one unit may be made available to other units. To some extent such information would travel along the usual informal horizontal channels, but a central coordinating group provides greater assurance that all units will have knowledge of activities in other areas. Greater government regulation of industrial relations matters, also has increased the need for coordination in the opinion of some companies. Increased utilization of the telephone and other mechanical means of communication has resulted in an increase in both the speed and the amount of communication among the plants of a company. This has increased the need for coordination, even while it has facilitated greater coordination.

B. Relation to Level of Decision Making and Corporate Structure

1. *Coordination*

The degree of centralization or decentralization of decision making concerning industrial relations policies determines to some extent what is involved in coordination. Where policies are centrally determined it is assumed that they are desirable for all units of the company. The process of coordination then is essentially one of ensuring uniform application in all units, and avoiding interpretations in one unit which might set adverse precedents for another unit. In the case of locally determined policy, coordination requires that management personnel in the various units take into account the possible impact on other parts of the firm of decisions made in their unit.

For purposes of analysis, three major aspects of coordination under centrally determined policies can be defined. First, it is necessary that supervision in the units understand clearly the policy and its objective. Second, since policies, even when accompanied by detailed procedures, frequently do not indicate an obvious decision in a particular application, it is important to develop a "philosophy of industrial relations" or a common approach among members of management who carry out the policy. Third, local units will require advice on the application of policy in specific cases despite the guides provided by the devices already discussed. In the absence of common rules for the whole corporation, coordination of locally determined policy requires more emphasis on developing a common approach. Depending upon how much locally determined policies differ, the need for day-to-day coordination of their application is somewhat less than for centrally determined policies.

The organizational structure also influences the amount of coordination required and, as indicated below, the problems involved in effective coordination. In some multi-industry firms with divisional organization on a product-industry basis, management, employees, and unions are more interested in comparisons with other firms in the same industry than with other divisions in the same company. Where organization is along functional lines there may be even less concern in, say, the manufacturing division about what is done in the sales division. Similarly, in some cases where wide geographical dispersion of plants exists, interest tends to be centered more on comparisons with regional or local labor markets than within the firm. It should be pointed out, however, that the notion that the firm should treat all of its employees similarly is a strong force and often prevails over such variable factors.

2. Control

A review of the application of industrial relations policies may be of a broad nature with the purpose of determining whether industrial relations in the unit concerned are progressing satisfactorily. This type of control would seem most compatible with decentralized decision making on industrial relations matters where the methods for obtaining satisfactory industrial relations are left up to local units. Although this broad type of control is not impossible under centrally determined policies, there is a tendency for review to become more detailed under the latter circumstances. Companies frequently referred to control as a procedure to check on whether or not specific industrial relations policies set at corporate headquarters were being carried out by all units rather than as a check on the general tenor of industrial relations.

C. METHODS OF COORDINATION AND CHANNELS OF INFORMATION

1. *Gaining an understanding of policies and contracts*

Whether centrally determined to apply to all units of a firm or locally established for a single plant, industrial relations policies and union contracts are common rules to be applied to individual incidents as they occur. The first step towards uniform application of a common rule is to ensure that it is clearly understood by the various supervisors who have authority to make decisions concerning its application. A number of the individuals interviewed stressed this aspect of coordination as the most important one in obtaining uniform application.

a. Written

One of the basic methods of obtaining understanding of policies is to put them in writing, usually in the form of a policy manual for members of supervision. Of the 41 companies in which information was obtained on industrial relations policy manuals covering the whole corporation, 27 had such manuals. Their widespread adoption is further emphasized by the fact that of the 14 firms which did not have manuals at the corporate level, two firms had them in some of their divisions, two had some policies in writing, and two others were considering establishing manuals.

Most manuals discuss the objectives and intent of each of the various policies of the company as well as providing a formal statement. In addition, procedures to implement the policies are usually included in the manuals.[1] Particularly in the case of company benefit plans which require some centralized application, procedures may be quite detailed. For example, plant industrial relations managers are given this sort of direction for carrying out the pension program of one company:

"Prior to the fifteenth of the month, the Pension and Benefits Section

[1] See Chapter IV, p. 57 for a discussion of implementation.

will advise the local employment point by letter to have the employee or pensioner appear at the local Field Office of the Bureau of Old Age and Survivors Insurance. . . .

"On or about the twenty-fifth of the month, Compensation Division will send a letter to the employment point for delivery to the pensioner informing him of the amount of his pension."

It is evident that setting out the steps to be followed in applying policy in so detailed a manner reduces the possibility of variation in its application.

That companies do not rely completely on manuals for understanding of policy is indicated by the distribution they are given among members of supervision. Widespread information on this matter was not obtained from companies surveyed, but it appears that about half the firms provide all levels of supervision with copies of the manual and the remainder send copies only to the plant manager or plant personnel manager. The comments accompanying information on manuals also suggested that manuals alone were not sufficient. For example:

> The manual is useful as a broad general guide. It serves as an adjunct to communications, but it is not communication *per se*.

> — — —   — — —   — — —

> Manuals must be continually revised and supplemented by verbal explanations.

Nevertheless, companies recognized their importance as a basic device for obtaining understanding.

Some of the companies also felt that manuals reduced the tendency for supervisors to call the industrial relations manager and cut down on the number of referrals to headquarters by plants. As one company, which distributed the manual to all levels of supervision, stated:

> The Manual gives such good understanding that only the most touchy questions are discussed with corporate personnel.

However, one plant personnel manager observed that even when foremen were given manuals, they still called the industrial relations department frequently because it was easier to pick up a phone than to look up a policy in the manual. Another executive felt that, although the number of referrals to the head office had not been reduced greatly after a manual was made available, the questions asked of headquarters became much more intelligent and specific.

In addition to manuals, letters and bulletins sometimes are used to obtain an understanding of policy. A number of companies use interpretive bulletins to explain more fully policies stated in manuals or to emphasize certain policies that have gained in importance since the manual was issued. Minutes of the meetings of policy-making groups are also circulated in some cases and looked upon as written records of policy.

b. Meetings

One of the most common methods of supplementing written statements of policy is a meeting of the various units of the company or the divisions in a plant in which either a line or staff member explains some part of existing policy or changes in policy. Regularly scheduled meetings of both the corporate industrial relations staff with subordinate staffs and of corporate management with line managers at lower levels were found widespread in the companies studied. In the 31 companies from which information was obtained on this matter, 15 reported regularly scheduled meetings of the corporate industrial relations staff with plant staffs, usually on an annual basis. Eight other companies held meetings of the divisional staffs with the headquarters group, and about half of them also held meetings of the plant staff with divisional personnel. Because the divisional staffs often were located in the same building as the headquarters staff, such meetings were more frequent than the plant-corporate gatherings.

Of the remaining eight companies, only two reported no meetings of staff personnel on a corporate or divisional basis. The other firms either utilize for this purpose their master contract negotiations, at which the industrial relations managers of all plants involved are present, or hold meetings irregularly or for only the plants in one locality which represent a preponderance of productive capacity.

Similar practices are followed for line meetings in which industrial relations matters are discussed. Only one of the companies reporting on this item does not hold such meetings. In some firms the head of industrial relations also attends these line meetings.

In addition to these general meetings, which are often utilized to obtain better understanding of corporate policies, a number of the companies reported the use of special meetings called specifically to explain contracts or industrial relations policies. Such meetings are often used for some complicated policy change such as a new benefit program or for explaining changes in the contract upon the completion of negotiations. A few of the companies with large industrial relations staffs also hold annual meetings of specialists at the plant level with the corresponding section of the corporate staff.

There is widespread use of meetings within the plant also. In the smaller plants they are not held frequently because informal personal contacts are thought to provide adequate means of transmitting information to all concerned. However, even in these cases, special meetings have been held to explain new contracts. In the larger plants weekly or semi-monthly meetings for general operating purposes usually are also used to discuss industrial relations matters.

Many of the people interviewed felt strongly that meetings are essential to understanding policy. This was particularly emphasized at the plant level. Commenting on the use of meetings, one plant superintendent said:

> When a new policy comes out I want to be sure that everyone is told what it means. New policies are explained either in the regular foremen's meeting or at special meetings. After explaining the policy it is necessary to ask the foremen if they understand it and then ask them to repeat it in their own words.

In the words of a corporate personnel director from another company, meetings are:

> the best way to obtain an understanding of policy and contracts because only when questions are asked can it be discovered what possible misconception supervisors have.

This particular company tries to keep meetings down to no more than 20 people in order to permit sufficient opportunities for all to ask questions.

The most common criticism of meetings was that they consumed too much time. It was also recognized by a number of firms that sole reliance could not be placed on meetings because of the possibility of misunderstanding without written material and of incomplete communications if some people were unable to attend the meetings.

In holding meetings, one of the questions that arise is whether the explanation of policy and contracts should be made by line supervision *via* chain-of-command meetings or by the industrial relations staff directly to the subordinate level of management attending. Some companies pointed out that explanation by line personnel was important to enhancing their status in the eyes of subordinates and also gave the subordinate a greater incentive to understand what was said.

On the other hand, some companies reported that when meetings for explaining policy or contracts were left up to line supervision, such meetings were not always held. Furthermore, chain-of-command meetings increase the number of persons who transmit the information and enhance the possibility of error. As pointed out in Chapter IX below, the industrial relations staff is almost always directly concerned with the formulation of policy and often attends contract negotiations. Therefore staff can give a direct explanation of the reasons for having the particular policy or contract clause as well as describe it. In some cases the members of supervision who were receiving the information reported that the industrial relations staff gave a clearer explanation.

From the standpoint of prevailing practice, the industrial relations staff seems to be favored over line for making explanations of policy and contracts. In the plants studied intensively, all but the smallest company, which in one plant had no industrial relations staff, used industrial relations department personnel for this task. Although information on this question was not sought from all survey companies, those who did report overwhelmingly favored using staff personnel.

c. Other methods

Informal methods such as personal contacts between plant and headquarters personnel *via* telephone, visits, or master contract negotiations are also utilized to obtain understanding of company policy and union contracts. A number of those interviewed felt that participation in negotiations was one of the best ways of ensuring that local people understood what the contract is intended to mean. That holds equally true for participation on unilaterally determined policies. In addition some of the companies felt it was important to keep local supervision, who could not participate directly in negotiations, advised of developments in bargaining so that they might better understand the meaning and intent of the final agreement. Explanation of policies and contracts also is part of most training programs for supervisory personnel.

d. Special practice for new plants

One special problem of interest in the category of obtaining understanding of policy is that of the newly acquired plant. If it is decided that corporate policies shall apply at the new location it becomes important that supervisory personnel be given an understanding of such policies as soon as possible. One of the most common methods of dealing with such situations is to transfer into the new plant as industrial relations manager someone from one of the corporation's already established plants or from headquarters. Thus there will be available to all supervisory personnel in the new plant someone fully acquainted with corporate policy. Where such a move is not feasible, frequent visits by corporate industrial relations personnel may be made to the plant and intensive personal training carried on for the plant manager and industrial relations manager of the newly acquired concern.

2. Obtaining a common approach in industrial relations

A number of the companies interviewed stated that a common philosophy of industrial relations was the most important aspect of coordination. The unique characteristics of every industrial relations problem, in their opinion, made it impossible to obtain uniformity solely by applying common policies, however well understood.

In obtaining a common approach, great emphasis is laid upon informal methods and attainment of the objective over long periods of time. The process begins with the selection of supervisory and staff people. Those chosen are "our kind of people." As pointed out in a description of one company:

> ". . . [coordination is obtained by] hiring and training men who share completely in management's outlook."

Indoctrination in company industrial relations philosophy is a continuing, though informal process from that time on. Much of it results from a kind of apprenticeship relation with superiors in the day-to-day handling of industrial relations matters. The process was expressed in one company in this manner:

> From the first assignment to management this indoctrination process begins. . . . There is a lot of tradition in a company that has existed so many years, and this tradition is passed on by a multitude of people with whom a man coming up through the ranks of management has contact. The ———— Company has an *esprit de corps* and a tradition very similar to that which is found in a college.

Interviews also revealed that positions of such importance as plant manager and, often, plant industrial relations manager were filled by individuals of long association with the company who had adopted the corporation's philosophy as their own. A number of firms placed great importance on such long association with the company, one stating:

> . . . we place much emphasis on having grown up in the organization and having a feel of what the organization means and stands for. For that reason, we have found out in the past that it pays us to take a man who is already in the organization and train him in some specialized field rather than to hire a specialist from the outside and try to teach him the feel and the understanding of the corporation as a whole.

Assigning personnel to headquarters for various lengths of time before placing them in positions of responsibility at plants is a slightly more formal method of assuring that the common philosophy is implanted in all personnel. A substantial number (12) of the firms interviewed reported such a practice. One company reported that:

the average experience at headquarters is eight or ten years before a man is sent out as a plant personnel manager. In this period the central staff can be sure that the man is fully indoctrinated with the company's policy on labor relations and that he is the type of person who will follow these policies. A similar practice is followed in choosing managers and even top level supervisors for outlying plants from among men in the home plant.

3. *Uniformity in day-to-day application*

Regardless of the use of other methods to obtain coordination, all firms relied heavily upon devices whereby local management could obtain guidance in the application of policies to specific cases. Written media such as arbitrators' decisions and grievance settlements are used by a few of the companies specifically for this purpose. On occasions, supervisory newsletters and other means for disseminating information in general are also utilized. The meetings described in Section 1 also provide an opportunity for personnel of different operating units to compare experience and thus increase the likelihood of uniform action on similar cases.

However, the most important method for obtaining uniformity is through a common source of advice on the application of policies to specific cases. The industrial relations staffs at both plant and corporate levels perform this function. The effectiveness of this method of obtaining uniformity depends on the degree to which cases not obviously falling under a specific policy are taken up with the appropriate industrial relations staff. Line supervisors almost invariably were quite willing to seek advice from plant industrial relations staffs. Similarly, plant industrial relations managers frequently consulted divisional or headquarters staff.

Consultation on individual cases creates the possibility of a great amount of time being taken up by such matters. However, few people interviewed complained of that aspect and almost all foremen replied that prompt decisions were obtained when cases were referred to upper echelons of management. Although they apparently had no unusual difficulties of this nature, two companies had organized their corporate staffs in such a manner that delays were likely to be minimized. These firms had established field representatives of the corporate staff in various geographical areas where a number of their operating units were located. Thus, immediate personal contact with the corporate staff was available to plant industrial relations managers.

4. *Coordination of local policies*

Even for those policies that are determined by the local operating units of the firm, some coordination is necessary. Local policies dealing with the same industrial relations problems often are quite similar throughout the company and require coordination in their application.

Essentially, the problem is to see that sufficient information is made available to local management concerning the industrial relations activities in other units and that local management takes into consideration the impact of its decisions on other units of the company. The problem is basically the same as under centrally determined policies except that local management is somewhat less conscious of the need for coordination. Hence, the methods of coordinating the application of centrally determined policies discussed in the two previous sections are applicable here, except, of course, as they relate to master contract negotiations.

Some additional devices are available to coordinate policy making on these locally determined items. One of the most frequent concerns of corporate personnel was that local management tended to become so interested in solving its own problems that it failed to think of the firm as a whole. One device used by a number of companies for overcoming that tendency is the practice of assigning plant personnel to headquarters for periods of duty or of transferring them among a number of plants.

a. Providing information on other company units

A number of companies circulate an industrial relations newsletter that summarizes important occurrences in the various plants of the corporation. Usually information for these newsletters is obtained from periodic (often monthly) reports to headquarters by the local units. Supervisory newsletters are also used in some cases to report developments in the various units of the company. Local plant newspapers also are circulated to other units in a number of cases.

Where collective bargaining is conducted by local personnel, the need to provide information on developments in other units is intensified if locals of the same international union are involved or if the various unions cooperate to any extent. Even though, as indicated in Chapter IX below, the important decisions are made centrally in many cases in which negotiations are conducted locally, it is still necessary to make sure that local negotiators do not put the company in an untenable position in discussions preliminary to final agreement on important matters.

Besides the direct participation of central staff in negotiations, a number of devices are used to provide information on local collective bargaining to all units. A contract in effect at one plant often is distributed to the other plants; formal pre-negotiation strategy meetings are planned at headquarters for local negotiators; or the corporate staff, by telephone calls and personal visits, discusses with local negotiators approaches that all might take to the coming negotiations. Once negotiations are under way, each unit has to be advised of significant developments in other units either through the direct exchange of information between plant managers or through the corporate staff.

b. Coordination of different divisions and with other firms

The coordination of industrial relations matters among different divisions of the same company and with other firms in the same industry or labor market are two special cases similar to that of coordinating policies that are locally determined. As pointed out earlier in this chapter, the industrial relation situations may be different in the various divisions of the firm, but the fact that workers of all divisions are employees of the same company means that some consideration must be given to coordination. The action of one company may have an effect on other firms in the same industry or labor market. Consequently the question of formal or informal coordination with other concerns as well as within the individual firm arises.

In general the companies interviewed did not put much emphasis on coordination among divisions. One of the case study companies has three functional divisions operating within the confines of a single company property, but depends upon informal coordination among local managers. The extent of coordination as described by those unit heads is to keep each other informed of what they are doing, or planning to do. None of them reported having to alter plans to avoid creating problems for the others. Had such a situation arisen and had local personnel failed to reach an agreement, coordination, it was stated, would have been obtained at the corporate level by divisional line management and the corporate industrial relations staff.

In another instance, eight plants representing several different product divisions of a large company were located within a 30-mile radius. Despite the fact that, according to the plant manager interviewed, action taken in his plant was known shortly by all other company plants in the area, formal efforts for coordination within the area consisted solely of bi-monthly dinner meetings of the top two levels of management in all plants in the area. Informal telephone calls were the principal means of exchanging information and experience.

In addition to the fact that quite different operations are usually involved in the various divisions and that different occupational groups may be concerned—for example, production workers and white collar workers—it should also be pointed out that different unions were involved in the various local operations in the two examples cited. In the case of the first company, much closer coordination was required at another location, where by historical accident marketing and manufacturing employees were represented by the same local union. Furthermore, in the same company, the timing of wage increases among units in different divisions was coordinated on at least one occasion to combat union strategy.

In the presence of an aggressive and alert union, the very diversity of industrial relations situations in the separate divisions intensifies the need for coordination. Under such conditions what may be an unimportant concession by one unit may set a very costly precedent for another. Similar problems occur in unilateral policy that management feels should apply to all units of the company.

Information on the subject of inter-company coordination was obtained from only a few of the cooperating firms. No formal arrangements, except where bargaining was on a multi-employer basis, were reported, but such informal devices as telephone calls and local management association groups were available. Individuals interviewed stated that coordination involved exchanging information on what had been done rather than attempts to obtain common action. Interest in coordination among different companies seemed highest where a number of firms in one industry were located in the same labor market area.

5. Comparative use of formal and informal methods

The replies to the question of what were the principal means of obtaining coordination indicate that informal methods are relied upon much more heavily than formal. Thirty of the companies interviewed (including three interviewed intensively) mentioned informal personal contact through visits or telephone conversation as the principal, or one of the principal means of coordination. In one form or another the statement that reliance was placed on "informal contacts between plant and corporate industrial relations staffs on a day-to-day basis" was found with great frequency. In contrast, only fifteen of the companies listed meetings, ten reported written methods, and four mentioned a common philosophy in reply to the same question.[1]

In the very large corporations with big divisions there was some tendency to depend upon written methods for coordination in the corporation as a whole, but even in these cases the divisions relied heavily on informal personal contacts. The common feeling seems to be that formal methods are not sufficiently reliable and often not rapid enough to keep up with the day-to-day need for coordination. As one industrial relations director put it:

Travel rather than committee and board meetings is the key to coordination.

Although as indicated earlier, reliance on day-to-day referrals to headquarters might result in a great deal of time being spent on such matters, in individual cases speedy replies can be obtained by telephone or teletype.

D. CHARACTERISTICS AND METHODS OF CONTROL

1. *Characteristics of control of industrial relations matters*

Control as audit should not be confused with the use of the term to include centralized decision making. For example, a number of the companies interviewed cited the required approval of plant contracts by corporate headquarters prior to final agreement at the local level as a control device. Although information obtained in that process can be utilized for control purposes, the requirement of approval before concluding the agreement is a form of decision making by headquarters.

As indicated earlier in this chapter, control of industrial relations matters may be either of two types: a test of the general tenor of industrial relations or a detailed check of the results of the application of specific policies. The latter involves policing to be sure that centrally determined policies are carried out as envisioned at headquarters. The greatest obstacle to the use of the former type is the difficulty of obtaining a reliable, objective indicator of the general state of employee and union relations. Perhaps the broadest test that might be used is the profitability of the local operation on the assumption that financial success depends upon employee productivity which in turn hinges on satisfactory employee relations. However, a currently satisfactory profit

---

[1] The total exceeds the number of companies interviewed because some companies mentioned two or three principal methods.

record may be achieved at the same time that relations with workers are suffering adverse effects which will be reflected only in operating data of the future. It is therefore not surprising that none of the companies studied used such a broad control.

Various other indices, such as turnover rates, number of grievances, and absenteeism, or combinations of similar, objective data, have been suggested as a measure of the state of industrial relations. However, few executives believed that such devices could provide sufficiently accurate control. Consequently, there was a tendency for the firms interviewed to look upon control as a process of determining the results of specific policies and of checking to see that policies determined centrally are carried out by the plants. In fact, because it is also often difficult to assess the impact of specific policies, emphasis is put on the latter aspect. Some variation of the following was a frequent comment on the matter of control:

> Corporate industrial relations has the job of policing the company to determine that policies are being carried out.

— — —   — — —   — — —

> "Something like the military inspector general is needed for industrial relations. Some control is necessary to make sure that the policies of the corporation are being carried out and that plants are not establishing policies in industrial relations which are not up to the standards that _____ would like to maintain."

In an area in which objective measures are not considered reliable and in which errors may have a lasting undesirable effect on a company's reputation, a desire for close control is to be expected.

In general, the companies interviewed did not seem to have a clearly conceived control program for industrial relations. Partly this seems to result from the difficulty of obtaining reliable, objective indicators as already discussed. In addition, in the minds of some people, control has a connotation similar to "commissar" and, as a result, there is some reluctance on the part of headquarters to develop a full-fledged program. Consequently, although the firms tended towards a more detailed type of control, the various devices available to carry out such a program often were not utilized intensively. With the exception of one company, the corporate industrial relations division was assigned to carry out whatever control measures were utilized.

2. Formal methods of control

a. Statistical reports

Although corporate management was not willing to rely heavily upon quantitative measures of the general tenor of industrial relations for the purpose of control, a majority of the firms collected statistical information on these matters on a corporate-wide basis. Such data could be utilized to check on the carrying out of policies and to analyze the results of the application of policies, as well as to help assess the overall situation in industrial relations. Twenty-nine of the 46 companies interviewed required statistical reports of some sort from their operating units. Sixteen of the reports were quite comprehensive. Data such as turnover, absenteeism, safety, benefits, wages, hours, etc. were contained in such summaries so that almost every aspect of industrial relations subject to quantification was included. The other thirteen companies collected statistical information on only a few items. The specific functions most frequently reported on in those cases were safety, wage and salary administration, and turnover.

It is interesting to note that many of the people interviewed commented that these reports and the narrative reports discussed below were not looked upon as control devices. For example:

> The purpose of these reports is primarily for an historical record, but they are also used for audit purpose although not in any systematic or routine fashion.

— — —   — — —   — — —

> A comprehensive monthly report is made by each plant industrial relations manager to the corporate industrial relations staff. . . . These monthly reports occasionally show something that needs looking into, but not very often.

Such an attitude is evidence of the lack of emphasis given to the nature of control programs for industrial relations.

b. Grievance procedure

The grievance procedure, which provides for union challenges of management's interpretation of the labor agreement, can also be used by corporate headquarters to check plant management's application of the contract. Information on grievances may be obtained either informally as a result of requests for advice by plants or formally through required steps in the grievance procedure involving corporate management or through mandatory approval by corporate levels of decisions to take a case to arbitration. Some of the companies studied achieved a broader coverage by having the plants report on all grievances that reached the final step involving plant management. Often that is done by sending the minutes of the grievance meeting to headquarters. In one company a spot check on grievances is utilized in which a local plant is required to report on the disposition of every case that arises in one month.

c. Personal audits

Six of the companies send representatives from headquarters to the plants personally to conduct audits of industrial relations. Such check-ups involve discussing recent problems and their solutions, surveying local practices and, in some cases, actually going through local employment and wage records and other data to see if company policies are being carried out. In general these inspections by headquarters personnel are conducted more in an atmosphere of trouble shooting than auditing. In fact, two of the companies stated that the headquarters representative making the audit reports the results to the plant manager only, and not to his superiors, and another only reports to a plant manager's superior if the plant manager gives his permission.

d. Other methods

A few of the firms use morale and employee attitude surveys that provide information of value for control purposes. However, such indicators are not used as a broad control device to permit more decision making on a decentralized basis. Rather, they seek to determine the effectiveness of centrally determined policies and the need for additional policies. In a few companies, headquarters checks plant manuals for deviations from corporate policy. Those few companies that do not require central approval before labor agreements are signed review the contents of the contracts which the plants are required to send to the home office.

3. *Informal methods of control*

As was the case for coordination, heavy reliance is placed on informal methods of control. Informal controls are not so obvious and thus lessen to some extent the atmosphere of surveillance of the formal devices. Probably the most important informal method of control is the personal visit to the plant by corporate staff personnel. As one executive pointed out:

> A general office man going through a plant learns a tremendous amount as to how these policies are being carried out. . . . One cardinal rule is that the general office man reports to the plant manager—not to the general office.

In another case, division line personnel are also asked to observe industrial relations practices on their visits to plants:

Whenever anyone from the production division visits a plant, he always reports to the entire staff of the division on his return, thereby ... giving the industrial relations staff a chance to coordinate the administration of personnel policies in case one of the plants is getting too far out of line.

At the plant level, the plant manager's or the industrial relations manager's personal contact with the employees is often considered the most important method of control.

In addition to its role in the grievance procedure, the union often is an informal source of information on how plants are carrying out the industrial relations policies of the company. This source is most likely to be available in cases in which the union bargains with corporate personnel, either on a company-wide basis or for individual plants, and where relations are amicable. The union often performs a similar function within a plant.

Other informal methods also supply information of use for control purposes. Any contact between the corporate staff and the plants, such as telephone calls for consultation or informal conversations at meetings, may bring to light deviations from corporate policy. Even the often unreliable "grape-vine" may indicate areas that need checking.

E. Problems of Coordination and Control

1. *Communications*

Communication is the life blood of coordination and control. It is, therefore, not surprising that the most frequently mentioned problem in this area was poor communication. Most of the usual obstacles to satisfactory transmission of information were mentioned by at least one of the executives interviewed. However, a few occurred so frequently that they require separate treatment.

Wide dispersion of plants throughout the country and the great distances between plants and headquarters were often cited as adding to the difficulty of communication. Although improved methods of communication have cut down the barrier of distance substantially, there are still costs involved. The emphasis on day-to-day coordination and on personal contacts *via* telephone calls and field trips as means of coordination and control magnifies the problem of geographic distances. Evidence that distance imposes some barrier could be seen in greater uniformity of practice among plants located near headquarters than among those at greater distances.

Another commonly cited problem of communication was that of

the size of the corporation. In this case, size referred to the number of plants primarily. The amount of coordination and control required depends upon the number of operating units determining and applying industrial relations policies. A combination of geographic dispersion and a large number of plants was found to result in considerable emphasis on these two points as obstacles to communication in a few companies.

A number of the people interviewed listed time as an important limitation on communication for the purpose of coordination. Some industrial relations personnel stated that they did not have time to make the field trips necessary for good coordination and control. In addition, decisions often had to be made before efforts to coordinate could take place. As one industrial relations director stated:

> . . . . communication remains the greatest weakness in coordination. It is always a problem of time versus the need for action. Immediate action may make it impossible to get information around and to get consultation prior to action.

Only a few companies reported reluctance to consult as an obstacle to communications. The head of industrial relations in one firm felt that an important cause of this problem was a feeling of insecurity on the part of some plant managers and the belief that requesting aid from headquarters would be interpreted as an indication of inability to handle problems on their own. In another case, a past history of local autonomy made plant managers unwilling to consult for fear of losing some of their authority.

2. Diverse local conditions

Obtaining uniformity in industrial relations matters is made more difficult for a large number of companies by diverse conditions in operating units. Those differences may arise out of methods of production, geographic location, state laws, or union situations. Although such dissimilarities might be expected to lessen the need for coordination, as pointed out earlier, there is a pervasive feeling that all employees of a company should be treated the same. Reports from the firms indicated that diverse state laws were perhaps the least problem of the differing situations encountered.

From the number of comments received, differing union conditions apparently were the most important diversity impeding coordination. In many cases plants were organized by different international unions. Not only do unions differ in their attitudes towards certain industrial relations policies, but often rivalry between unions may result in one trying to outdo the other. In addition, even when all plants are organized by the same international union and bargaining is company-wide, a particularly aggressive local on occasions forces plant management into strained interpretations of a master contract.

3. *Acceptance of centrally determined policies and their coordination*

Another problem frequently referred to was the failure of local management to recognize the need for and the importance of coordination. Statements such as the following were encountered frequently:

> The chief problem of coordination is the inability of plant managers to recognize interests above those of their own needs. These plant managers must learn to consider the company-wide effect of their actions.

Indoctrination, training at headquarters, and other methods of developing a sense of stewardship in an enterprise broader than the single plant or division were undertaken primarily to avoid this problem.

The coordination of industrial relations matters requires not only that supervisors who are to apply centrally determined policies and union contracts understand their meaning and objectives, but also that lower levels of management do not disagree so violently with the policies and contracts that they either reject them or modify them in the process of application to specific cases. Participation in the formulation of centrally determined policies and contracts, as described in Chapter IV, is one way of increasing the likelihood that lower levels will accept them. That is true not only because, as a result of participation, lower levels will feel they have had a part in making the decision, but also because policies and contracts so determined are more likely to fit the needs of the local situation.

Acceptance of union agreements may also be promoted, it appears, by giving lower levels of supervision some idea of the reasons why management accepted a given contract. This may be achieved both by keeping first line supervisors informed of developments in negotiations as they take place and by explaining the contract, clause by clause, after it has been signed. The flow of information on developments in collective bargaining was one of the areas in which lower levels of line supervision were most critical of top management. Many first line supervisors felt that management did not tell them enough about developments in negotiations and that the union usually got the information to employees and shop stewards before management informed plant supervisors. Partly this is the result of less effective communications by management than by the unions. However, part of the problem is management's reluctance to supply such information for fear that what they say of a confidential nature may leak out and either put management at a bargaining disadvantage or raise false hopes in the minds of some employees. The union can be less concerned about the latter effect since they can always claim that management refused to grant the demand.

F. Appraisal

1. *Tendencies towards centralization*

The emphasis placed on informal personal contacts between the corporate industrial relations staff and plant management and the considerable amount of consultation on specific cases provide frequent opportunities for the corporate level to take part in decision making in the application of policies. It is, of course, impossible to determine to what extent the ultimate decision is made by higher or lower levels of management in such circumstances. However, the very process of advising lower levels of management of the proper interpretation of policy often results in the corporate staffs leaving little to decide concerning the application of policy.

To the extent that the formal publication of a company's industrial relations policies eliminates the possibility of local units having their own version of what constitutes company policy, some power to make decisions locally is lost. The inclusion of detailed procedures for the carrying out of company policy also limits the discretion of plant management.

Even in those instances in which policy is locally determined, the need to consult with headquarters on whether the decision in question will have adverse effects on other plants involves an element of centralized decision making. Plant management has little choice if it is advised by the corporate staff that the contemplated action would not be in the best interest of the company. Plant personnel interviewed stated that they rarely were forced to forego local programs because of the possible effects on other plants, but it should be pointed out that unique conditions existing in the case study companies minimized the need for coordination of locally determined policies. Three of the four companies dealt with different unions in their various plants, which were widely dispersed geographically. The fourth company operated under a master agreement with only minor matters left to local option.

The heavy reliance on the industrial relations staff, at both the plant and corporate level, in obtaining coordination tends to enhance the

status of staff personnel at the expense of line. This is particularly true
at the plant level where frequent referrals to the plant industrial relations manager are the chief means of coordination and where staff personnel are often used to explain new contracts and changes in policies
to lower levels of supervision. The reduction in prestige of line supervision may result in more decision making at top echelons of management instead of at middle management levels.

Although less obvious than the methods already discussed, the development of a common approach, or a company philosophy, also is a
tendency towards centralized decision making. The common approach
is established by the actions of top levels of management and is emphasized by the indoctrination of lower levels both by precept and
example. It is highly significant that the development of a company
philosophy as a method of coordination avoids the problem of the time
element in coordination.

The process of control can be important to permitting decentralized
decision making if reliance is placed on audits of results rather than on
a check of how centrally determined policies are being carried out. In
the absence of any reliable method of measuring results in industrial
relations, however, the control exercised by headquarters staffs has
tended towards checking on the carrying out of policy and thus has
decreased the amount of leeway that plant personnel have in the application of policy.

2. *Factors encouraging decentralization*

The increased emphasis on informing plant management of developments throughout the company promotes decision making at lower
levels in two ways. In the first place, plant management is given information without which it might be unable or unwilling to make decisions on local matters. In the second place, the passing on of such
information is taken as an indication that higher levels of management want lower levels to make decisions utilizing that information.

The detailed descriptions of policy and copies of contracts enable plant
management to make its own decision on application. The existence of
a manual may also indicate what areas are open to local policy determination. In a few cases where a strong personality at the corporate
level had dominated industrial relations throughout the corporation,
the introduction of a manual was looked upon as "the substitution of
rule by law for rule by a man" with the implication that there was at
least a little latitude in the interpretation of "law" by the local plant.

RESPONSIBILITY FOR DECISIONS

ON SPECIFIC SUB-FUNCTIONS

VI. THE LOCATION OF RESPONSIBILITY FOR MANPOWER UTILIZATION

I N the final analysis, any evaluation of centralization and decentralization must come to grips with certain questions regarding how and by whom specific decisions are made. For example: What decisions or what phases of decision making can, without undue risk, be delegated to the plant manager, the department head, or the foreman? What decisions must be centralized at a high level for the good of the corporation as a whole? Do certain functions continually lend themselves to a greater or lesser degree of decentralization or does the practical extent of delegation of responsibility for any given function depend on variable factors?

In this and the three following chapters, an attempt is made to answer these questions in the light of information received regarding the location of responsibility for specific activities covered by the term "the industrial relations function." The analysis of reported differences in delegating responsibility for these specific items also gives insight into the characteristics of a given activity that may determine how and at what levels policy is most successfully made and applied.

A. MANPOWER PLANNING AND EMPLOYMENT

1. *Policy determination*

Manpower planning involves the projected determination of the number and kind of people required in an organization. It is forward looking, giving breadth and guidance to the more limited and more exact development of policies for and the functioning of employment, promotion, and training activities. The employment function is, in part, an extension of manpower planning into the smallest units of the organization, but also, in part, a more integrated function. Employment procedures may, and often do, go on from day to day without any general consideration of the corporation's or the plant's future manpower needs. The nature of manpower planning and of the actual processes of employment would seem to influence the former towards centralization and the latter towards decentralization. In fact, however, manpower planning often exists only as employment planning and procedures at the plant level, and certain employment policies tend to be centralized at the corporation level for reasons other than those related to the determination of future manpower needs. Moreover the hiring process, which was once the responsibility of the foreman, gradually has become centralized in the plant personnel department, or even in the headquarters industrial relations department for certain types of applicants.

The information received on this subject suggests that the term "manpower planning" is often used only under circumstances that make it particularly difficult for the corporation or one of its plants to recruit the needed manpower. Top management attention is then given temporarily to consideration of emergency policies or to assignment of responsibility for developing policies and procedures. The fact that only 17 of the 46 companies supplied information on manpower planning, that several of these replies dealt wholly with employment policies and procedures, and that several companies reported the discontinuation of manpower planning at the end of World War II indicates both the emergency nature of such planning and the common failure to distinguish between it and employment policies and procedures.

Among the 17 companies giving explicit information on responsibility for manpower policy, the responsible group in 10 companies included top management personnel (the president, or a committee, or membership of corporate officers on the board of a subsidiary), in four, responsibility was at the division level, and in three, the plant manager or the local industrial relations manager was responsible. The reports from companies where policies were made, participated in, or approved by a corporation executive or committee give the best clues as to the conditions that make manning problems of sufficient importance to require top level consideration.

Only one company reported the present use of a special manpower committee. This company, with more than 50,000 employees in widely scattered plants, seeks to operate on as decentralized a basis as possible. Headquarters has come to recognize, however, the inadequacy of supervisory and executive training in many of its plants and hopes to persuade its various divisions to give more attention to these problems. The recruitment of technical graduates previously handled independently by the divisions is now coordinated through the headquarters industrial relations department, and starting and progression rates are made uniform. The special manpower committee includes representatives from the corporation and the divisions. Its function is to cooperate with the corporation industrial relations department "in the coordination of technical, professional, and executive manpower planning and recruiting." The committee helps the industrial relations department develop policies with respect to management personnel and at the same time provides an excellent channel through which the corporation can "sell" its recommended policies to the divisions.

In other companies where manpower policies were considered by the president or the executive committee or operating committee of the corporation, the type of policy determined at this level was in some cases general, in others, specific and narrow. In one instance the division manager and his staff are nominally responsible for manpower planning, but special plans or policies must have the approval of the president. In others, corporate attention, involving the industrial relations staff and officers of the corporation, has been given to manpower planning in connection with product model changes, seasonal fluctuations, and (as in the company mentioned above) the recruitment and development of technical, professional, and executive personnel. In a few companies, need was expressed for more careful manpower planning in a search for greater stability of employment, sometimes influenced by union demands for guaranteed annual wages.

All of the cooperating companies gave some information on the levels at which employment policies are determined. Of the 46 companies interviewed, 29 (63 per cent) reported the participation of corporate level personnel in the determination of at least certain employment policies, in four participation or approval went as high as the division, and in only 13 (28 per cent) were both employment policies and procedures wholly the responsibility of the plant manager and plant industrial relations department.

An important reason for the frequent concern of the corporation with employment policies is that they must be integrated with many other personnel policies. As soon as applicants become new employees, expectancies are created and the corporation begins to assume long range responsibilities for fulfilling these expectancies.

Employment policies reported as established on a corporation or division-wide basis include: minimum and maximum hiring ages, requirements and standards for physical examination, the employment of members of minority groups, citizenship requirements, and recruiting of technical and professional personnel. Companies with such corporation-wide policies often permit plant managers to make decisions as to the use of tests, educational requirements, and other employment procedures or standards not covered by a corporate statement. In general, plant management is given much more leeway in employment policies applicable to rank and file than in those applicable to specialists and managerial personnel. At least a number of the 13 companies stating that employment policies were wholly the responsibility of the plant were referring only to the rank and file and lower level managerial employees, since they also reported that college recruiting was centralized and selection or promotion above a certain job level required approval higher than the plant manager.

The most common procedure reported in the development of corporate employment policy was formulation by the head industrial relations staff after consultation with the division and plants, and with final approval by a chief executive or committee. Policies are then announced by an executive letter or as an addition or change in an industrial relations manual. Policy making on the division level consisted in some cases of approval of policies recommended by the corporation industrial relations department. In cases where different production problems and different unions dictated different employment policies, the divisional industrial relations staff is likely to be responsible for policy recommendation and the division head may give final approval. However, even in such multi-industry corporations certain employment policies were commonly accepted by all plants even if not put into writing, since corporation-wide pension and benefit plans encourage standard physical examinations and some adjustment of hiring age to the requirements for retirement benefits.

2. *Responsibility for the application of policy*

As far as application of manning or employment policy is concerned, the coordination of activities and, to a considerable extent, the actual procedures involved in employment are a staff responsibility. The responsibility of the corporate industrial relations department is usually limited to the implementation of policies by procedural manuals, except for special classes of employees (such as engineers, chemists, industrial relations and other staff personnel), when the actual recruiting and hiring may be handled by or coordinated through the headquarters staff. Common practice is for headquarters staff to recruit these specialists, but to leave the definite selection and placement to the plant manager, division manager, a higher executive or to joint decision by staff and several line executives.

The employment section of the plant industrial relations department bears the principal responsibility for recruiting, hiring, and placing rank-and-file workers. The plant medical department is responsible for physical examinations. Nominally, in most plants, the foreman or department head has the right to reject applicants chosen by the employment office. In practice, such rejection has become infrequent for production employees of large plants. This is felt to be the result of the tight labor market, career employment with a frequent practice of hiring into a common labor pool, and promotion from within on a seniority basis. Most of the foremen interviewed took these practices and centralized employment for granted, and there were few specific complaints concerning the lack of opportunity to select their own workers. Maintenance foremen often have a more active part in selection of their men, since skilled mechanics must frequently be hired from the outside and the maintenance supervisor still considers himself the best judge of an applicant's previous experience and skill.

Various aspects of the inter-relation of headquarters and plant, and line and industrial relations staff within the plant, are seen in the description of employment procedures in one plant:

> Specific standards for pre-employment physical examinations are established by the plant doctors who know the physical requirements for each job. However, the headquarters division has issued a book on company medical practice which sets up general standards. The plant has recently begun to use a few employment tests. Before they were used, the plant employment manager consulted with the test expert at headquarters. Decision to try the tests was made by the plant manager, the industrial relations manager, and the department heads concerned.
>
> Almost 99 per cent of the plant operators are hired into the labor pool and the line supervision has no part in the selection. The employment supervisor makes the original selection and turns the new employees over to the foreman of the labor pool. Promotion from the pool is made on the basis of seniority. When skilled people are hired from outside, the supervisor involved interviews the applicant. In the case of stenographic and clerical personnel, the clerical supervisor usually interviews the applicants before they are hired.

In this company, as in many others, the employment function is centered in the plant employment office with changes in procedure requiring the approval of plant manager and the plant industrial relations manager. The effectuation of employment policies appears to extend from the plant staff upward into the headquarters staff to a greater extent than downward into plant supervision. Headquarters not only sets standards for plant procedures, but it also exerts an influence on plant practice through its consultative services. In addition it actually handles the employment of certain specialized personnel. For certain groups, such as skilled mechanics and office workers, the supervisors may still have some voice in selection. Frequently, however, plant supervisors no longer participate in the selection of the individuals whom they supervise.

B. TRAINING AND PROMOTION

1. *Policy determination*

a. For rank-and-file employees

The levels at which training policies are developed and carried out vary principally according to the type of personnel involved. Training in the sense of teaching an employee the necessary skills for a specific job is almost wholly a local matter. Unlike employment policies, any corporate statement with respect to the training of plant operators is likely to be in the most general terms. There are two principal exceptions to this: apprenticeship training for skilled craftsmen (which is often determined through collective bargaining) and programs "to help an employee understand a plant's problems."

The latter is frequently called "adult education in industry," or "economic education of employees" and represents a comparatively new and broadened concept of the training function. One company expresses the objectives of its expanded program of training and education as follows: "to change the individual's total behaviour—his skill, his knowledge, his understanding, and his attitude." The result of this new concept is to raise the level of policy development in the "education of employees" to top management, in contrast to the continued delegation of "training" to the plant level. Even in this one aspect of training and education the actual decision as to the adoption of a program is usually left to the division or the plant management, although the impetus towards establishment of a program is considerable when it has been developed by the headquarters industrial relations staff at the request of the executive committee.

Participation in the determination of promotion policy for plant operators was reported to reach as high as the division or corporate level in 70 per cent of the companies interviewed. But like training policies for rank and file, promotion policies are stated in very general terms. Corporation policy in this area, for instance, may consist only of a statement to the effect that all units are expected to follow a policy of promotion from within, and that individual advancement takes into account both ability and seniority. However, implementation of these policies through personnel rating as well as their direct application in selection for promotion is so extensively delegated to the plant level that, in practice, the policy often varies considerably among the different plants. In the opinion of many, the complexities of seniority and the tendency to accept seniority as the principal basis for promotion of employees covered by a labor contract tend to nullify policies that seek to establish other bases for promotion. Thus, unlike the majority of personnel policies studied, promotion policies for non-supervisory employees appear to be more decentralized than written statements of policy generally indicate.

b. For supervisors, executives, and special management personnel

Top management's interest in supervisory and executive development has increased markedly since the 1939 survey of industrial relations policies. Such interest is expressed in planning and even in participation in training more than in stated policies. The decision as to whether there shall be a distinct executive development program and the form it will take is almost invariably top management's—after consultation with the headquarters industrial relations staff and line executives at the divisional level. The decision to encourage supervisory training is now frequently a top level matter. Actual planning of the supervisory program is sometimes done by the training section of the headquarters staff, but, among the group of companies studied, the installation of a supervisory training program is still left to the plant manager and plant training supervisor more often than explicitly set up by the division or headquarters level.

One vice president explained the lack of policy statement in spite of his president's strong belief in supervisory and executive training as follows:

> Training must go from the top down and should start at least with the plant manager. There is a psychological resistance to training as such and it is necessary to camouflage it as preliminary planning and as seeking the participation and advice of line executives. The management committee and supervisory conferences are both a means of management training.

Perhaps partly because such psychological resistance does not apply to new recruits for management or prospective management personnel, statements are more frequently put into writing with respect to the training of college recruits or recent graduates employed for technical, professional, or junior executive positions. A training program of this type is usually determined at the same level at which college recruiting is handled, that is at the division or headquarters level.

Promotion and transfer policies for supervisors and executives were found to be of interest to top management in the majority of reporting companies, although like employment policies for rank and file, they were generally stated in such broad terms as "an opportunity for the development of each individual to his fullest capabilities." Because of the infrequent statement of policy either with respect to supervisory and executive training or promotion, the extent of corporations' present interest in this field is best revealed in the implementation and administration of policies.

2. *Application of policy*

a. For non-supervisory employees

The actual training of production employees and plant office personnel is with few exceptions carried out at the plant site by plant line personnel. The principal exceptions are: induction of new employees; training by the corporation or division training staff when plants are located near the staff offices; and the broader education included in adult education programs. Advice and suggested programs are frequently provided by the headquarters training staff on all phases of training and their influence tends to result in more uniformity than might be expected from the decentralized training procedures. The extent of this advisory service is indicated by the existence of corporate training staffs in over one-half of the companies studied. The nature of the consultative service and functional coordination was explained by one executive as follows:

> The central headquarters employee relations department is in the same position as an outside consulting agency would be. They try to sell the plants on the advantages of the various types of training plans, and they suggest to the plant manager what they think he needs in the way of a training program. However, it is up to the plant to accept or reject these programs.

This statement suggested considerable plant autonomy, but was modified by the further statement that

> If headquarters feels strongly enough about the need for a certain training program in a plant, they can talk it over with the divisional head (who is located in the same building), and if they can convince him, pressure could be put upon the local plant manager.

Considerable functional control is exercised by the plant training staff in most of the large plants. In addition to giving advice and suggestions to the supervisors, the training staff handles some of the actual training. This is particularly true of certain parts of induction training of new employees and of the newer type of educational programs. In spite of the active role of the plant training department, it was interesting to note that supervisors interviewed felt that training was their responsibility and that the training staff gave them little assistance in this function. It appeared that on-the-job training, almost always the responsibility of the foreman, was, in the foremen's eyes, the largest part of the operator's training.

The selection for promotion of non-supervisory employees is also primarily the responsibility of plant line organization. In about 75 per cent of the companies surveyed, consultation with respect to these decisions was reported not to go beyond the plant level; in the other 25 per cent of the companies, plants may consult the central staff on procedural matters, or the divisional level may be involved in cross-plant promotions. None of the companies replying to the short questionnaire require approval by headquarters of non-supervisory personnel. Within the plants, any decision to promote other than according to seniority is jointly determined by several levels of plant supervision. Such cases are usually also discussed with the union to avoid a grievance. Occasionally, the advice of the personnel director and the plant manager also is sought.

The roles played in decisions on promotions appear to depend upon the relative weight given to ability and seniority. In general, the greater the weight given to employee work performance and personality characteristics, the greater is the influence of lower supervisory levels. While no situation was encountered where an employee's immediate supervisor had final authority to promote, where ability was taken into account the supervisor's appraisal was always considered by those who made the final decision. The information received in this study suggests that situations in which equal weight is given to ability and seniority are becoming rare.

b. For supervisors

The central industrial relations staffs in about three-fourths of the survey companies reporting on this subject are involved in the development and administration of supervisory training programs. The chief functions of the central staff were shown to be to develop programs, encourage their use, and provide other kinds of assistance to the plants where the bulk of training is conducted.

This assistance is more extensive than that provided for non-supervisory training. One additional function that is performed, for example, is the training of plant discussion leaders. The implications of such a procedure to the question of centralization were expressed by one executive as follows:

Last year, we hired a man who acts as corporation training director. His function is to promote supervisory training activity at all plants— economic education as well as other activities. On the face of it, this would appear to be a step towards centralization—but then, a man is also trained in the local plant to do a job. The latter is responsible to the plant manager. That raises questions as to whether it is centralization or not.

To the extent that such training combines definite, prescribed subject matter with specific training techniques, a degree of centralization is indeed involved. The central training of people to head up plant supervisory training programs was seen as an attempt both to develop a somewhat uniform level of supervisory information and skills and to indoctrinate supervisors with those value judgments felt to be necessary to insure "sound" and "safe" local decisions. The ultimate objective of such training may be to allow for more decentralization within prescribed limits which supervisors have learned through centrally initiated training procedures. As reported above, the plant part of this training may not be called training, but may be a part of the regular meetings of plant managers and supervisors in which headquarters personnel participates from time to time.

The direct training of supervisors is handled centrally in at least six of the 46 companies interviewed—all of them with 35,000 or more employees. Some of these supervisory training schools are organized on a formal basis and housed in separate buildings. Other companies conduct a less formal type of central supervisory training. One company, for example, does the following:

> Several foremen from each plant have an opportunity to visit the central office. They are given talks by the industrial relations department and division management (located in the same building) on such subjects as products produced, planning, sales, customer promotion, labor relations and public relations. They have an opportunity to visit the chart room, the board of directors room, the original company site . . . and the country club.

The administration involved in the operation of the central training is primarily the responsibility of the company training staff.

Although in the majority of reporting companies the supervisory training programs are carried out without direct assistance from headquarters, the bulk of the formal training is conducted by the plant personnel staff rather than by the line organization. Not only does the staff handle such matters as planning and scheduling, but it also does much of the teaching. On-the-job supervisory training (principally informal) is still a line function, but orientation for new foremen, human relations training, courses "aimed at getting supervisors to accept their industrial relations assignments," discussions of labor contracts, and economic education programs are chiefly conducted by the local training staff.

In some companies, there is considerable collaboration between the staff and the line with respect to programs designed to improve the ability of supervisors to answer employees' questions about the company and its industrial relations policies. In one plant, such a program was led jointly by a department head and a staff training supervisor. The speakers for the program were drawn from both line and staff personnel.

The promotion of rank-and-file employees to first line supervisors is chiefly a function of higher plant supervisors. In one plant in which supervisory responsibilities were analyzed, such decisions were found to be made by either the department head or division head. Selections are usually made from lists of potential foremen compiled from information supplied by foremen and general foremen and/or in consultation with them. Where employee appraisal records are kept, the foreman potential of employees is noted. Such record keeping sometimes results in greater centralization and in a greater voice for the personnel staff. In the plant referred to above, a new program was recently developed which calls for the following:

> The plant training supervisor and the employment supervisor go over the list of potential foremen made and compare them with a man's past records and his background and then have all this information available when an opening appears for a foreman. To some extent, this method is used to encourage the selection of foremen on a plant-wide basis rather than just a departmental basis. The department head, however, still has the final say.

c. For executives and other management personnel

The corporation industrial relations staff and its training specialists are as important in the planning and coordination of executive development as plant staff is in the coordination and handling of supervisory training. However, corporation executives play a much more active role than do division or plant executives in supervisory training. A number of companies pointed out the responsibility of the head industrial relations manager (in contrast to his training staff) in organizing and supervising executive development and the participation of headquarters or divisional executives both in planning and carrying out the program. Those companies that mentioned executive participation in special management development courses offered by universities stated that selection of company representation was made by a top level executive or committee with the advice of the industrial relations staff and division heads.

Promotions to plant and division executive positions almost invariably receive central management attention. Headquarters also reviews promotions within or into supervisory positions in a substantial minority of the survey companies. Forty-nine (55 per cent) of the companies answering the short questionnaire stated that headquarters' approval was required for promotions below that to plant manager as follows: for all promotions into or within supervision, 17 companies; for key management personnel, 9; for a few of the plant manager's staff, 4; unspecified, 19. In one of the survey companies, the executive committee reviews all promotions of men to "pivotal" positions. In another company, the selection of persons to the rank of plant manager is made by the vice president in charge of manufacturing, with the approval of the president. The head of a division in one company said the following about intra-plant promotions:

> Although I depend primarily on the plant managers to know whom to promote, I personally take an interest in plant staff positions—the positions of manufacturing and technical superintendents, for example. I have an opportunity to know something about the candidates through my long association with the plants and I exert my viewpoint concerning their promotion.

Both the assistant general manager and the manager of one of the division's departments added that they kept close track of transfers and promotions down to plant people in the $500-$600 per month category. Sometimes the division industrial relations staff makes the initial decision as to whom to promote. Such division interest in plant promotions was confirmed by one of the division's plant managers. He said that he consults with the division on the appointment of department heads because the division wants "to keep track of" the outstanding young men in the company.

Generally speaking, the chief interest of the central staff in intra-plant promotions is to facilitate the upward flow of the most promising people by making promotional opportunities available on a broader base than to the group of employees who happen to be in the unit in which the opening occurs.

As reported in Chapter III,[1] the corporation industrial relations

1 See p. 44.

office usually exercises some degree of influence in the selection of division and plant personnel staffs. One company director of employee relations described the sharing of responsibility as follows:

> We make recommendations but the actual selection is made by the plant manager. We may even tell them who they ought to hire, but it's up to them to decide.

Similar participation in the selection of personnel for plant counterparts of other headquarters staffs was also reported. Whether the promotion is to plant manager or his staff, the selection to positions at this level is of importance to the present and future welfare of the corporation as a whole. The majority of companies studied recognize this fact and want, on a formal or informal basis, one or more persons with a broader view than that of the single plant to participate in the choice.

C. Discharge and Layoff[1]

The making of policy and administrative decisions with respect to discharge and layoff situations has four chief characteristics: policy is established at a high level (although specific procedures are usually made locally); it is one of the best examples of the application of line-staff joint action; decision making is diffuse, with group decision making a common practice; and some aspects of these functions are almost always subject to collective bargaining.

Management's right to discharge employees was one of the first to be challenged by unions. Union surveillance and challenge, together with protection under the Wagner Act and the Taft-Hartley Act against employees being discharged for union activity, has led to greater attention to this area by higher levels of plant management and by central management. Especially where management actions hold implications for company-employee and community relations, central management is interested. Another influence toward centralization is the possible financial cost involved in discharges and layoffs that may not be upheld by an arbitrator or government agency.

The chief limits to centralization and influences toward decentralization are the need for immediate action and the need to be acquainted with the details of a case. The need for immediate action can be combined with fuller and higher level consideration of a particular case through the procedure that the foreman send a man home on indefinite probation and that final action be deferred for a specified period of time.

[1] See also "The settlement of grievances and decision to arbitrate," Chapter IX, pp. 159-162.

The need for detailed information about individual cases can also partly be compromised with centralization. Such information can be put in writing and considered at higher levels. Supervisors, however, often lack the ability to write a clear and adequate description of the situation.

1. *Policy determination*

In about 85 per cent of the survey companies, changes in policy in regard to discharge and layoff are primarily determined by the central industrial relations staff. Consultation downward, in the development of company-wide policy, was reported less frequently than required approval of interpretation of policy by headquarters' staff or a high level executive. Such top management consideration of policies seems to have been delegated more fully to the central industrial relations staff since 1939, for at that time these policies were found to be "generally determined by the chief executive or executive committee on the recommendation of the director of industrial relations and an advisory committee." This is not surprising since discharge and layoff policies are now fairly well standardized and policy decisions are more frequently modifications of established policy.

Policies generally made at the headquarters level include the following: (a) the amount of and conditions under which separation pay is allowed; (b) refund of separation pay in case of reemployment and the relation to continuity of service; (c) causes for discharge; and (d) certain general procedures to be followed in case of discharge, such as the requirement to conduct an exit interview.

Although only about ten per cent of the survey companies said that they completely delegated policy determination in this area to the plant level, most companies reported some policies that were locally determined. Chief among these are the seniority provisions that determine the order of layoff, and particular procedures for discharge, such as a system of formal warnings or the use of formal discipline and discharge committees. Many of these policies are subject to collective bargaining.

2. *Application of policy*

As suggested above, decision making with reference to the handling of discharge and layoff situations offers one of the best examples of the diffusion of decision making over several levels of management, of group decisions, and of the line-staff relationship. An analysis of the various steps in the process illustrates the complexity of the centralized and decentralized nature of the discharge and layoff function.

The initiation of a decision to discipline or discharge an employee is the foreman's task. The second step in the decision-making process is to recommend specific action or alternatives. Preparing a recommendation for as serious a matter as discharge may involve the assembling of all relevant information and consultation on the interpretation of policy or labor contract. The plant industrial relations staff nearly always, and often the corporation staff, enters the discussion. Local procedure usually prescribes that the plant industrial relations staff be consulted on any discharge action where there is doubt that the case would stand up under appeal. The headquarters staff is consulted especially on matters of interpretation. Such consultation was described by one corporation industrial relations director as follows:

> The plants have come to learn to check with corporate personnel before discharging a man because of the arbitration case which is likely to follow. It is also often necessary to consult headquarters on discharge and layoff because of the need for interpretation of the corporation's dismissal compensation plan.

It is after, or in conjunction with, such consultation that recommendation for definite action is taken. In a few cases, it is the foreman himself who recommends action, but, more often, higher levels of supervision or a committee is involved. An important measure of the extent of delegation in disciplinary action is how seriously the foreman's recommendations are taken. One foreman claimed that top management had never overruled a foreman on a recommended discharge. A general foreman in the same plant said:

> Although the foreman and general foreman cannot discharge a man, their recommendations are important to the decision of whether he will be discharged or not in a discipline case. It is left up to the foreman and the general foreman's judgment as to when there is no hope of straightening out an employee who has been a discipline problem and when discharge procedure should begin.

The procedure involves fewer people when less severe penalties are concerned. The right of a foreman to place an employee on 30-day probation was accepted by a few companies in the case of a serious violation of rules. In some companies the foreman has the authority to discharge new probationary employees. Even for flagrant violations, however, most companies advise the foreman to send a man home and to refer the matter upward. Not a single company reported that a foreman had the right to make his own decision to discharge a regular employee. In every company, several people from different levels or departments of the plant were involved, and in every company the plant manager or plant personnel manager was party to the final decision. A union representative is often brought into the decision-making process early in the discussion. One plant reported the use of a board of inquiry.

Decisions involving layoffs generally are more centralized and less diffused than those concerning discharge cases. Sometimes the decision is handled at the corporation level; at other times, depending upon the number involved and expected length of layoff, it might be made by the plant manager.

Decisions reached by plant management are not necessarily final, but often require further approval or review by the division or corporation level. The head industrial relations staff frequently must approve the dismissal of salaried employees above a certain income level or of both salaried and wage employees of more than a given length of service. Review may be synonymous with required approval and permit the reversing of decisions, or it may be only a matter of being kept informed of all dismissals and, perhaps, calling questionable decisions to the attention of those responsible for them. The reviewing officer may be the plant industrial relations manager, the division head, or the corporation industrial relations manager.

An illustration of review that resulted in the reversal of a dismissal made at the plant level was given by a company director of industrial relations. He told of an instance in which 16 men had been discharged for intimidating a supervisor. The industrial relations director disagreed with the plant manager, and the consequent discussion between plant and headquarters executives and staff resulted in the decision to take back several of those who had been discharged. The director still thought this was not centralization since "the procedure was so handled that the plant manager knows he made the final decision."

The influence that review has on voluntary consultation prior to a decision is hard to estimate, but it is felt to be considerable. While no company had the formal requirement for review above the corporation industrial relations staff, two companies stated that discharged employees sometimes wrote to the president. The effect of the possibility of this occurring more frequently was described by one division industrial relations manager:

> Although there is no requirement that long service personnel not be discharged without checking with headquarters, the plant manager knows that long service people might write to headquarters if they are discharged for any but a very serious offense. And this is the type of corporation where a member of the board of directors or one of the vice presidents or president would actually check up on any such letter.

Plant managers know that they must be prepared to explain why a man could be with the company so long and then have to be fired.

D. Factors Affecting Levels of Decision Making in Manpower Utilization

Policy decisions for the group of industrial relations functions included in this chapter are predominantly centered at headquarters. Procedures in the application of policies are predominantly the responsibility of the plant line management or personnel staff. However, it has been seen that one or another or several levels may be responsible for a particular policy decision or its application. One fact stands out: personnel decisions for the functions considered in this chapter are rarely made by one person or one level of management. Instead, decisions are diffuse, in most cases involving referral upward or consultation downward or both.

The principal level at which a given policy is made or specifically applied depends on varying circumstances. The following six factors have some influence in all of the functions just discussed, although their influence is much greater in some activities than in others. All are items that management might well review in determining the extent to which these policies and procedures should be centralized and to what extent they can safely be delegated.

1. *The importance to the corporation of the employees involved*

Decisions concerning management personnel are inevitably made at a high level. To some degree the present and future success of the company depends upon effective and careful selection, training, and placement of each member of management. Foremen are included in this category in all the companies interviewed. But because foremen frequently spend most of their working lives in one plant, procedures concerning them are, to a considerable extent, centered in the plant manager with consultation with higher levels on problem situations or special plans. In contrast, the selection, training, and transfer of specialists from whom future executives may come are commonly guided from headquarters.

2. *A special interest of top management*

This factor may or may not coincide with the long-run corporate good considered in the preceding paragraph. A president or executive board may change its interests in specific subjects or functions, or a new president may want to give more or less emphasis to certain activities. Thus a chief executive or committee may urge the adoption of a specific type of executive development or some form of "economic education" for employees and supervisors, or the proportional employment of minority groups. It is clear that the initiation of an activity at the top has considerable weight in encouraging adoption by subsidiary units.

3. *The possible impact of a given policy on other personnel policies and other units of the corporation*

A guiding principle in the delegation of responsibility for any personnel function is that other policies, and the impact of the new policy on other plants and on the corporation as a whole must be considered whatever the level at which the decision is made. A new employment policy may need to be weighed in the light of its possible effect on the cost of employee benefits. The selection and training of specialists and prospective executives must take into account a policy of promotion from within. The corporation industrial relations director is in a position to see the interaction of personnel policies most clearly, and he is most frequently depended upon to formulate these policies or to review, for inconsistencies and conflicts, those adopted at the division or plant level.

4. *Conditions outside the control of the company*

Among outside conditions that may affect the need, on one hand, for a company-wide program or for differences among the plants on the other, are federal and state labor legislation, business conditions and the state of the labor market, unionization, the strength of the union or unions with which the company must deal, the type of bargaining, and community attitudes. The principal impact of these factors is on policies applying to unionized employees and others in the production units. However, the condition of the labor market may tend to centralize the actual employment of specialists and to encourage some centralized coordination of other employment procedures that are handled at the plant level according to the community situation.

5. *The extent of the financial risk involved*

On-the-job training may be delegated to the foreman not only because he knows the job best but also because the cost of inadequate initial training on production jobs may not be as great as would be the costs of centralized job training. However, the company has more invested (in present salary and in plans for the future) in a specialist, and training for him usually is directed from the corporation or division level. Discharge of any except probationary employees may be costly business, and thus decision to discharge a worker even in the lowest job grade may be a matter for consultation with the plant manager or a higher executive.

6. *Employee and executive attitudes*

Employee attitudes have been of increasing interest to top management in recent years. Thus, discipline and discharge decisions are reviewed at a high level not only because the union may appeal and an arbitrator may reverse the foreman's decision, but also because of the ill effect of an unfair decision upon other employees. Interest in an employee's attitude towards the economic system as well as towards the company has encouraged the installation of programs of economic education. Attitudes of management personnel have affected both terminology and procedures. Executives do not like to be lectured to or to be "trained." These are factors in the use of the term "executive development" and in emphasis on consultation and conferences rather than on formal training sessions. A foreman's dislike of reversal of his decisions and the effect of such reversal on employee attitudes have also influenced the growth of extensive consultation prior to announcement of decision.

VII. WAGES, SALARIES, AND HOURS OF WORK

A. GENERAL WAGE CHANGES

1. *Policies*

ALTHOUGH policies of some sort form the basis for company procedures with respect to the "when," "how," and "how much" of general wage changes, the findings of this survey suggest that these policies are more frequently a matter of common understanding than a written guide. The matter of most concern to the companies studied was not, it seemed, that wage policy should be understood but rather that the decision in every case should take into account possible repercussions in all units of the corporation.

In the companies in which policy was referred to, it was stated that decision on policy was made at the corporation level. Management's keen interest in this subject was indicated by the fact that in two-thirds of these companies the decision as to underlying policy was made by the president, the executive committee, or the board of directors. In the other one-third of these companies, the chief industrial relations executive nominally established the policy for plant action. However, a number of these executives stated that under certain circumstances they would consult the president or executive committee before approving action contrary to established policy.

The lack of clear distinction between policy and specific decision was evident among many of the companies providing information on general wage changes. It might be assumed that the companies failing to report any central policy as to wage changes permit such policy to be set at the plant level. The stated requirement for approval at the corporation level of all general increases suggests, instead, that any policy that provides a framework for general wage changes is usually determined by a few key executives who can act promptly in permitting the adjustment of past practice to immediate needs.

2. *Responsibility for specific decisions*

All information received with respect to the responsibility for general wage changes indicated that final decisions were made by or near top management. Of the 89 companies responding to the short questionnaire, 85 stated that headquarters must approve such changes. Of the 45 companies interviewed on this matter, only two stated that decisions were not referred beyond the division level.

In one of the companies in which final decision is made by the division, corporation officers are members of subsidiary boards and represent the corporation point of view in the decision made by the subsidiary. In the second company, no major group of employees is unionized. The remaining 43 companies with whom this question was discussed reported three principal types of corporation activity in a general wage change: (1) Some one or more chief executives make the final decision. Those mentioned were the president, the executive committee, or the board of directors. The corporate industrial relations manager and the head or heads of the subsidiary units affected are involved in the preliminary discussion. (2) The corporation sets a maximum percentage increase and the local management may bargain within that limit or over how much of the increase will be allotted to direct wages and how much to fringe benefits. (3) The corporation industrial relations head and others at headquarters are consulted before final decision is made at a lower level.

It is difficult to estimate the extent of corporate influences when consultation between plant and corporation is the normal procedure. Nominally when increases are made plant by plant, the plant manager recommends the increase and makes the final decision after consultation. But consultation of several levels of management and their industrial relations staffs usually begins sometime before negotiations are scheduled and the plant manager is well acquainted with top management's point of view. At one time, one plant of a company, or one company in the industry may be the leader, and the other plants or other companies may simply follow the pattern thus established. At other times, a corporation may deliberately seek to avoid following a pattern. Corporations whose plants represent a number of industries may in the course of a few months practice all three types of top level participation mentioned above. Much depends on the bargaining situation.

Variations in the role top management and lower levels play in determining a general wage increase are illustrated by the following reports of practice:

Consultation

One company stated in its questionnaire return that "general wage increases are approved at [subsidiary] Company level in consultation with Corporation level when necessary. Administration at plant level. Subject to negotiation [at plant level]."

In the interview with this corporation's industrial relations director, an instance was cited when consultation failed to change a recommended increase, and another instance when it did. A particular plant wanted to make an increase considered excessive by the corporation industrial relations staff. The matter was referred to the subsidiary company of which the plant was a part. A meeting was held at which the plant superintendent, works manager, vice president in charge of operations for the subsidiary, and a representative of the head industrial relations staff were present. The recommended increase was allowed to go through on the basis that the employees' expectations had been aroused for a substantial increase. In another plant of the same company, the plant superintendent and his industrial relations manager consulted headquarters relative to a general increase for salaried employees. In this case, the plant executives were persuaded to decrease the amount they had first thought of offering.

Plant decision within an established limit, except for special problems

The manager of industrial relations of another company reported: "There is a ceiling on wage changes, but the plant managers can make changes within limits. However, if a plant manager faces a strike because of a wage dispute, he would have to consult [headquarters] before making a decision. We had a situation where the union tried to whipsaw seven plants by forcing a wage issue in one. The plant manager was told he must take the strike. There are thousands of variations of wage problems. We just try to roll with the punch."

Corporation decision for some plants, plant decision for others

The plants in the principal industry of a third corporation are given no leeway in general wage changes. These are negotiated by the corporation industrial relations head on a multiplant basis. Other plants follow the wage levels of the community, except one which is organized by the same union as the plants covered by the master contract. The vice president of industrial relations stated: "We are resisting the trend towards uniform rates."

Role of plant, division, and corporation levels in a wage decision

The questionnaire returned by the division of one company stated: "The Plant Personnel Manager recommends general increases, according to local conditions, which in turn are reviewed and approved by the Personnel Department. General wage increases which are subject to union negotiations are also subject to the approval of the Director of Personnel [of the Division]."

In a later interview this Director of Personnel explained further: When large costs are involved, such as a general wage increase, the division personnel department must get permission from the corporation. However it would still be up to the divisional personnel director to make the specific decision since corporation approval is expressed in X dollars per year.

The above illustrations of company practice all show two points in common: (1) whatever the usual assignment of responsibility for general wage increases, the corporation is an interested party that either is involved from the beginning of a discussion or steps in when the situation becomes critical; (2) a general wage increase even in a single plant often involves both line and industrial relations staffs at the plant, the division, and the corporation levels.

B. Planning and Maintaining the Wage Structure

The internal relationship of individual job rates within a plant and among the plants of a corporation is a more detailed, complicated, and continuous function than the matter of changes in the general level of wages. Maintenance of the wage structure involves primarily the processes of formal job evaluation and determination of wage scales through negotiation. Negotiation may be on the basis of an established job evaluation plan or for labor grades determined by historical factors and bargaining strength. Incentive rates must be related to the wage structure but are not always determined at the same level as job evaluation.

As in the case of general wage increases, policy decisions and administrative decisions often overlap. There is, however, greater need for the participation of lower levels of management in the maintenance of the wage structure than in overall wage changes. Greater variation is possible and inter-plant differences in the wage structure often exist even in the case of multiplant bargaining. Nevertheless, reported practices indicate an increasing management effort towards the centralization of job evaluation and wage administration.

1. *Policy determination*

Policies relative to a company's wage structure may be established on a corporation, division, or plant level unilaterally by the corporation, or jointly by management and a union or unions. A company may state the broad guiding rules for determining basic rates in all its plants (such as to follow community or industry practice), or it may encourage its plants to adopt job evaluation or decide to establish one central plan. Whether such a policy can be put into effect depends to a considerable extent on the attitude of intermediate and lower levels of management and of the unions involved. Similarly the corporation may express a preference for hourly or incentive wage payment systems, but the adoption of one or the other or a combination is likely to be subject to bargaining.

Approximately one-third (14) of the companies interviewed have a job evaluation scheme for wage earners set up on a company-wide basis. An additional nine companies reported central encouragement of job evaluation with assistance offered to the local plants. "Encouragement" in the case of job evaluation seems less compelling than in certain other functions. This may be the result of the essential need for local cooperation in the establishment and administration of a plan or of the existence of historically important differences among the different plants. In any case, job evaluation or an incentive system cannot be put into effect by top management as of a given time and then forgotten until the next wage negotiations.

For example, one company that had developed job evaluation for its production workers over a period of several years reported that:

> "The company has experienced difficulty in the administration of wage plans because of the failure of local unions to appreciate the necessity for the application of standards in practice as well as on paper. . . . the original job evaluation scheme has been distorted beyond recognition. What exists is a series of more or less loosely constructed procedures at each plant varying within the broad limits set by the master contract."

This and other similar experiences reported by a substantial number of companies suggest that even when top management goes to great length and expense to establish a corporation policy and program, the nature of the problems involved tends to modify centralized policy and to strengthen local determination.

2. Administration

Wage administration, like the development of wage policy, appears to be in a continual state of conflict between centralized arrangements to maintain consistency among plants, on the one hand, and the unavoidable decentralizing influence of local day-to-day decisions, on the other. More than half of the companies interviewed had some degree of centralized administration of wage rates. A few were extremely centralized. Uniformity or some degree of consistency was maintained by means of various procedures. These included: (1) a uniform job evaluation plan, coordinated through a special staff in the headquarters industrial relations or industrial engineering department; (2) centrally negotiated or approved labor contracts establishing rates for specific grades or classes of labor; (3) a uniform wage incentive scheme using time study men trained and supervised by the central industrial engineering department; (4) the centralized approval of plant wage budgets (thus limiting a plant's total expenditure on wages while permitting variation in the wage structure); and (5) the requirement that individual wage changes beyond the established grade rate be approved at the corporation level.

The following procedures were reported by two companies with highly centralized wage administration:

"Matters Requiring Finance Committee Approval
"Changes in Employee Compensation
"(1) All Increases and Decreases In Pay To Individual Employees except those provided for under an approved Union Contract or automatic progression wage or salary scale. . . .

"In submitting [request forms] for increases to individuals whose job classification has an established rate range, the salary or hourly rate recommended must not exceed the maximum of the range approved by the Finance Committee unless the [form] also contains a request for sufficient increase in the maximum of the range. . . .

"Authorization request for increases in pay will be assumed to have been provided for in the latest budget approved by the Finance Committee unless a statement to the contrary is made in the [request].

"(2) All New Union Contracts And Any Negotiated Changes In Existing Contracts Whether Or Not Such Changes Affect Wage Rates.

"Subsequent adjustments in wages may be made pursuant to the terms of an approved Union Contract without Finance Committee approval *with the exception of proposed merit increases.* In this connection, all employees in the bargaining unit, whether or not members of the Union, shall be treated on the same basis.

"(3) All Changes In Basis Of Paying Commissions. (Such requests should be accompanied by an estimate of the total annual commission earnings to be payable under the proposed basis.)

"(4) Writing Off Unearned Advances To Employees Against Commissions. . . .

"(6) Establishment of Any Automatic Progression Wage Or Salary Scale Based On Length of Service.

"Subsequent adjustments in pay may be made pursuant to the terms of such an approved wage or salary scale without Finance Committee approval."

"Wage administration is under the industrial engineering department which is under the vice president of manufacturing. The industrial relations staff felt that since the industrial engineering people had to set wage incentives, they also should set the base rate. However, the corporate industrial relations staff has a veto without appeal by the industrial engineering division on any base rates that are set up. All new job rates that are set in the plant must be cleared through corporate industrial engineering and corporation industrial relations before they are negotiated with the union."

The second company just quoted believes in a high degree of centralization in industrial relations matters. The first company, however, aims to have considerable decentralization in this function, but cited many problems that made extensive decentralization impractical. The corporate personnel director explained the development of their centralized wage administration and experience with it as follows:

Government regulation played a great part in the establishment of this program in 1941. At first, the plant managers griped about the red tape, but griping almost ceased as the procedure became more automatic. It is now handled by secretaries both at the plant and headquarters' level. . . . The philosophy of the union seems to be to level off rates. This philosophy has upset the gradation of wages that was established. This distorts the wage structure. . . . Wages have ceased to be a matter of scientific determination and have become a matter of bargaining. . . . We have situations where the plant manager does not agree with our [the corporation's] wage policies. Sometimes we just have to say, "Do it this way."

An executive of a subsidiary also referred to War Labor Board regulations as the cause of this extreme centralization, but he was critical of its continued use, calling it "an unjustified expense and a waste of time."

Two of the least centralized situations found in wage administration were as follows:

In the one company whose plants are all in the same industry, the setting of individual rates is done locally. The most the corporate staff of industrial engineers has done is to suggest procedures to be followed. Piece rates for similar work differ from one locality to another. The union has not objected because there are fewer differences in job content now and also because the oldest and strongest locals have the best rates.

In the second company, one job evaluation plan had deteriorated, and a new one that was developed in one unit of operations has been recommended to all plants by the manufacturing department. Plant response has varied. The only pressure put on plant management is of an indirect sort showing the need and convenience of formal evaluation in case of rate changes, especially involving union negotiation. When a plant decides to adopt job evaluation, headquarters recommends one type of plan and offers assistance in developing it. A plant committee is expected to use the manual prepared by headquarters but may not want any further help. A plant with no evaluation program may be required to make a wage survey of community rates for a given job or jobs to justify an exceptional increase.

In this second company centralization relative to the wage structure is a matter of example, encouragement, advice, and being kept informed. Plant managers consult the division or the head industrial relations staff on these matters but feel that decision on changes in wage structure is primarily theirs and responsibility for the way a situation is handled wholly theirs.

The majority of companies interviewed stand, in the degree of centralization, somewhere between the examples cited above. In most cases, the initiative in the formalization of a wage structure comes from headquarters, assistance is offered in the development of a plan, and corporation policy is controlling in determining the basis for pricing the jobs. Establishing the plan may be done by local management alone or with the assistance of headquarters staff or outside specialists. The responsibility for maintaining a plan is, in some cases, divided between headquarters and plant, the highest level involved in administration being the corporation industrial relations staff; in others the responsibility for administration is wholly at the plant level, resting on both supervision and industrial relations or industrial engineering staff. Several companies reported union cooperation in the setting of rates in job evaluation.

One plant manager suggested that the handling of individual increases within rate ranges is probably the most decentralized activity associated with money matters. However, such increases are often closely regulated by procedures that prescribe the time interval when increases may be made and the amount of the increase; the only decision left to supervision is whether the wage increase is to be postponed or to be speeded up, when the contract permits even this much variation. The initiative for such a limited decision generally lies with the foreman and general foreman since they are in the best position to know a man's qualifications. According to the foremen interviewed their recommendation is usually accepted, although recommendations must be approved by the general foreman and department head. The department head might ask further questions to make sure that increases are not given too easily.

These comments of supervisors show that they feel that their decisions in rate changes are important, even though quite limited. A similar attitude was revealed by the plant manager of a company with a corporation-wide uniform scheme of job evaluation. Men from the head industrial relations department did much of the work of installation and they continue to analyze jobs before rate changes become effective. Nevertheless the plant manager feels that these men are his assistants while in the plant and that the wage rate must have his approval.

As suggested above in the discussion of policy, most companies expect some local variation in rates even though a corporation scheme is in effect. Centrally established rates may have to be modified to meet the peculiar circumstances of a given plant. Moreover, job changes are not always reported and local wage surveys are often inexact and can be used to justify whatever plant management wishes to recommend. The maintenance of consistency in the rate structure of one plant or among the plants of a division or the whole company requires coordination and the authority to make decisions by special staff or wage committees. The supervisors' acceptance of the program and their cooperation in it are of equal importance. Job evaluation, perhaps as much as any other single industrial relations activity, demonstrates the inherent strength of decentralization. Top management interest, a centralized program carefully developed by experts, extensive centralized controls, and even union-management agreement do not seem adequate to maintain a consistent and systematic wage structure for a long period except with the cooperation of plant supervisors and local union representatives.

C. Salary Administration

Salary administration is frequently handled by a different department or committee from that responsible for wage administration, and the findings of this study indicate a higher degree of centralization. Two-thirds of the 21 companies giving sufficient information to make a direct comparison possible showed that decisions with respect to individual salaries were made at a higher level than decisions with respect to the wage structure and individual wage changes. It should be pointed out, however, that some companies without formal company-wide position evaluation programs may establish the rates of office employees with no more or even less centralization than wage rates. In this area, the greatest contrast in level of decision making is between individual salary changes for managerial employees and individual wage changes for production workers.

The three principal reasons given for the greater centralization of salary administration were: (1) Salaried employees looking forward to a career in the company may face many transfers. Corporation-wide rates for the same jobs are important in facilitating moves from one unit to another. (2) Since salaried employees are less frequently union-ized, the company is freer to set up position evaluation for salaried people than job evaluation for wage earners. (3) The corporation has a special interest in the individual development of many of its technical, professional, and other managerial employees. Therefore, with or with-out a position evaluation scheme, it wants promotions and salary changes for these people to be considered by some individual or com-mittee that can view the personnel needs and goals of the whole cor-poration.

The differences between wage and salary administration lie both in the more uniform rate-setting for salaries and in the more frequent requirement of head office approval of individual salary changes. As one company reported briefly:

> "The plants set their own rates for new jobs but they must be ap-proved by the operations manager of the manufacturing department. There are no merit increases for hourly rated personnel. . . . We have a company-wide salary classification system. Merit increases for sal-aried personnel must be cleared with the home office."

1. *Policy decisions*

Among the decisions which establish policy on salaries for a com-pany as a whole are those with reference to: (1) position evaluation plans—whether one should be set up, who should develop it and who administer it, and what positions should be included; (2) the basis for setting rates—community, industry, or corporation-wide; (3) over-time pay for supervisors; (4) minimum differential between foreman and wage earners; (5) the amount and form of any general salary in-crease; and (6) how a general salary change is to be timed in relation to a general wage increase.

None of the companies referred to union bargaining on salaried mat-ters, except when they were included in the general phrase "all em-ployees included in the bargaining unit." An examination of agreements reveals that some cover unionized wage and salary employees in the same statement relevant to company evaluation plans, others refer to two different plans. A number of companies pointed out that office and other plant salaried employees not in the bargaining unit are often af-fected by wage negotiations. In companies with company-wide or divi-sion-wide bargaining, the decision for a general salary increase is al-most invariably made by the same top management group that has final decision on negotiations or by close collaboration of salary and wage committees. Where local bargaining was maintained, the policy of centralization of salary determination sometimes was found to be in conflict with the policy of decentralized bargaining, insofar as it was also considered desirable to relate office salary changes to wage changes in a given location. This conflict is avoided by some companies by including only "exempt" personnel in the salary evaluation plan and having other salaries handled at the plant level. In any case, decisions on general salary increases were seen to involve consultation among plant managers, division heads, and the executives at headquarters concerned with industrial relations, salary administration, and with the manufacturing or sales units affected.

The individuals or committees concerned with salary decision of a policy nature include variously the president, treasurer, corporation industrial relations manager, the special salary committee, executive committee, and board of directors. When both wage and salary policies are established at the corporation level, the final decision often is made by different individuals or different committees. For example one company reported as follows:

"A Salary Advisory Committee is responsible for the formulation and final decision on salaried personnel policies. The members of this committee are the Vice President and Treasurer—Chairman, the Executive Vice President, the Vice President and Controller, [two plant managers], the General Sales Manager, and the Director of Industrial Relations.

"The policies . . . for hourly personnel are formulated by a Labor Advisory Committee composed of the following members—the President, the Director of Industrial Relations, [two plant managers] and the Labor Relations Manager."

The company director of industrial relations was the individual most frequently mentioned in decisions on salary policy. Discussion often showed, however, that the industrial relations director's role lies in formulating and recommending policy rather than making the final decision. Salary committees, the next most frequently mentioned, include chief executives and the industrial relations director and usually have the authority to make decisions. When final approval must be made by the president, executive committee, or board, such approval is almost automatic because of overlapping personnel.

2. Administrative decisions

Specific decisions on both rate and individual salary changes are, according to this survey, made or approved at the top level for all or a large proportion of a company's salaried employees. Replies to the short questionnaire gave the clearest picture of the extent of centralization of individual salary changes. Out of 89 companies replying, 68 stated that all salary rates were set at headquarters, two that salary rates of supervisors and higher management personnel were thus determined. With respect to individual salary changes for plant personnel, 78 of the 89 companies reported a requirement for headquarters' approval as follows:

All salaried employees	19
All supervisors and higher	5
All exempt employees	4
Approval required for salaries above a specified level (ranging from $3,600 to $15,000 with half mentioning $6,000 or a lower level of inclusion)	28
Headquarters approval required (no statement as to the groups included)	22

More detailed information from the companies interviewed revealed the roles played by the operating unit or the division and that played by the head salary administration office. The reported experience of two companies just beginning a job evaluation program for salaried personnel suggests the problems of a previous high degree of centralization in the one, and the problems of considerable decentralization in the other. Both companies have announced an official policy of management decentralization. The personnel manager of the former company reported:

All plant salary and wage budgets must be approved by the president. He has recently requested that these budgets be routed through the company personnel department. The personnel manager goes over the budgets and if recommendations are not in line with what he thinks they should be, the president will not approve. The effort is to get each plant to make its own community surveys and to offer real evidence that it knows what community rates are before the budget will be approved. . . .

— — —   — — —   — — —

A plan for a uniform salary administration scheme is already under way. The president now approves all salary increases that involve annual salaries of $5,000 or more. When the salary administration plan is in effect, we expect to give more leeway to plant managers and to have control through the system rather than through approval of individual increases.

A divisional personnel manager of the second company stated:

Heretofore there have been varying degrees of decentralization. Because of the greater decentralization of certain small operating departments, some of their technical and managerial jobs have paid more than similar jobs in larger units. This made it extremely difficult to promote from the smaller department to a more responsible but perhaps lower rated job in a larger department. To overcome this weakness, a centralized salary administration plan is being established.

Job evaluation manuals for salaried employees show the high degree of centralization involved in such programs. For example, one manual describes the principal administrative function of the offices and divisions as writing job descriptions and keeping them up to date. The headquarters salary administration office is given responsibility not only for advice and coordination, but specifically to—

"Evaluate all job descriptions independently of the evaluation of the Division and to reconcile its evaluation with that of the Division and with ratings of similar jobs in other Divisions.

"Prepare salary analyses and other informative data for the Divisions in order that they will be currently informed on all matters affecting the administration of salaries.

"Conduct salary surveys with the assistance and advice of the Divisions.

"Prepare and maintain on a current basis Salary Schedules for all Divisions.

"Review salary increase recommendations for conformity with company policies and established practices."

D. Hours of Work, Vacations, and Holidays

The three subjects considered together in this section vary somewhat in the degree of centralization and decentralization followed by the cooperating companies. Weekly hours of work are most uniform, due to legislation perhaps more than company policy. (It is not unusual, for example, to find an interpretation of the Fair Labor Standards Act as the only material under "hours of work" in a company policy manual.) Vacation plans are highly centralized; holiday practices least centralized. All of these subjects are included in labor agreements, which fact of itself is an influence towards centralization. However, in a substantial number of companies, the top policy-makers had given consideration to one or all of these subjects prior to unionization. When unionized, these companies have continued to maintain a corporation-wide policy for unorganized employees and, as far as possible, to have such policy incorporated into their labor contracts.

1. *Policy decisions*

Of the 46 companies interviewed, all but one gave information on the level of decision making for hours, vacations, and holidays. In these 45 companies, 31 reported that standard daily and weekly hours were determined at corporation level, 7 at the division level, and 6 at the plants. Other aspects of hours of work were more frequently within the jurisdiction of plant management. Different processes and variations even within a given plant often require decision by those responsible for plant operation. Thus it was found that the length of the lunch period, the number of shifts, and use of overtime were almost invariably matters for decision by plant management. The degree of centralization for hours within a company may vary not only according to the particular aspects of hours of work but also from time to time. One company with more than 100,000 employees reported, for example:

> Hours of work are the responsibility of the local plant management and supervision, dependent upon production requirements. However, at times, the Corporation as a whole may determine to work longer or shorter hours on a regular schedule. At such times the determination is the responsibility of central management.

Policy in respect to vacations and holidays indicated an even greater degree of centralization for these than for hours of work. Thirty-nine companies reported that policy for vacations and holidays was established by the corporation, seven by the division, and four by the plant. When vacations and holidays were considered separately it was evident that vacation plans are more highly centralized than determination of the number of holidays.

Companies continue to make a strong effort to negotiate a uniform vacation plan into all of their labor contracts. Some, but not as many, try to maintain a uniform number of holidays with pay while permitting a limited variation in the particular days to be taken as holidays. Even with a uniform vacation plan (specifying amount of vacation for given years of service, how to determine service qualifications, and similar matters), divisions or plants may be permitted to decide such questions as the period within which vacations may be taken, or the time of plant shutdown, if all vacations are to be taken at one time.

Vacation plans for all salaried workers or at least for "exempt" employees are almost invariably established on a division or corporation basis. Holidays for salaried employees in plants are likely to be the same as for production workers. Holiday pay policy is commonly negotiated for unionized employees, but, like other wage policies, is subject to top level approval whether applicable to union or non-union employees.

2. *Implementation and application of policy*

Both policy and implementation of policy in hours, vacations, and holidays are developed by the corporation industrial relations staff and approved by a chief officer or an executive committee. The detailed application of policy is, of necessity, the responsibility of the plant, often being delegated to the plant supervisors. Supervisors are expected to consult with the plant industrial relations manager on matters of interpretation. If the locally determined policy or the application of a corporation-wide plan is thought to affect other plants, the plant industrial relations department will consult with the division or corporation industrial relations staff.

Interpretations of policy are sometimes spelled out in such detail that consultation on the application of policy to specific cases is reduced to a minimum. One company's manual includes the following statement concerning the administration of the plan for wage roll employees:

"The direct responsibility for the administration of this Plan is vested in the management of each employment unit. Management is given sufficient discretionary authority to enable them to meet local conditions or to work out unusual cases in a fair and equitable manner so that the purpose of the Plan and the promotion of sound industrial relations will be accomplished.

"However, it is desirable that any Company-wide plan of this nature should be administered with as much uniformity as practicable and in conformity with one general policy so that the employes of any one plant or department will not be treated with more or with less liberality than the employes of another.

"[Headquarters] INDUSTRIAL RELATIONS DIVISION should be consulted with respect to matters involving the interpretation and the administration of the various provisions of the Plan which are not fully covered herein or which may hereafter arise. . . ."

The manual includes a separate section on vacations for salary roll employes giving both basic policy and interpretations.

"*BASIC POLICY*

"The statement of basic policy which governs vacations for salary roll employees is contained in an Executive Committee Resolution dated April 22, 1953, which reads in part as follows:

"RESOLVED, that all Department Heads be advised that it is the sense of the Executive Committee that salary roll employees be granted vacation privileges no less favorable than those granted wage roll employees by the 'Vacation Plan for Wage Roll Employees';

"The following interpretations of basic policy should govern the granting of vacations and vacation allowance to salary roll employees. . . ."

The manual then proceeds to give in considerable detail interpretations of the plan as it should be applied to salaried employees.

E. Factors Influencing the Level at Which Decisions Are Made

The activities discussed in this chapter are, in general, more centralized than those discussed in the previous chapter. The greater centralization does not lie in policy making, which is highly centralized for all the individual activities considered thus far. Rather it is in the greater number of administrative details handled at the corporation level. However, within each of the activities covered in this chapter were found certain problems on which decisions tended to be made at a high level of management and other problems that tended to be solved at the plant level. A number of the factors influencing the level of decision making are the same for the several activities although their impact is of varying importance.

The principal influences reported and observed on the level at which wage and hours' decisions are made were as follows:

1. *Circumstances outside the control of the company*

Three principal factors were mentioned under this heading:

(1) The extent and type of unionization. Unionization was seen to be an influence towards centralization although companies maintaining bargaining on a local basis were attempting to counteract this influence. Unionization and multiplant bargaining appear to have a greater effect on centralization of decision as to rates and the wage structure than on overall wage changes. Whatever the extent of unionization or the level of bargaining, top management either makes or approves decisions concerning general wage and salary changes.

(2) Legislation and government agencies. A centralizing effect results not only from uniformity required by law, but by the fact that interpretations for plant practice are made by legal counsel at the corporation level.

(3) The size and condition of the labor market. The same factors

are at work here for centralization as were observed in relation to recruiting and employment. It is possible to generalize with respect to
different types of labor that the wider the labor market and the greater
the competition for labor, the higher the level of company decision as
to hiring rates and individual increases.

2. The costs involved

Individual rate changes or merit increases for wage earners involve
small amounts of money as compared with general increases. Similarly
one additional holiday in a single plant is less costly than an additional
week's vacation after five instead of ten years' service. Thus, merit
increases often and holidays sometimes are allowed to be determined
by plant management, while general wage increases and vacation plans
are almost invariably determined at headquarters.

3. Importance of jobs to the corporation

Technical and managerial personnel practices—especially salaries—
require top level approval, if not initial decision, for a number of evident reasons: the effect of salaries on indirect costs, the need for a
reasonably uniform salary structure in order to facilitate transfers between plants, and the desire of the corporation to be kept fully informed
on all aspects of the career of prospective executives.

4. The relative importance of local considerations and company-wide uniformity

This is one of the dilemmas of decentralization: To what extent can
local needs be controlling without threatening corporation policies and
standards? An example of a workable compromise is seen in connection with decision making for holidays. The *number* of holidays is
nearly always a matter of corporation-wide policy; the *specific days* to
be taken as holidays may vary according to local custom. Wage questions are more difficult since both industry and local rates may vary
somewhat from predominant practice in the corporation.

5. The number and frequency of decisions

When decisions must be made frequently on an individual basis,
centralization in the application of a policy is impracticable. Lower
levels of supervision are expected to be responsible within limitations
set up at a higher level and with varying degrees of coordination and
control. Assignment of individual vacations is handled by the immediate
supervisor and department head within the detailed rules of a specific

company-wide plan. A foreman's willingness to accept responsibility for reporting job changes that occur irregularly, however, may depend on the regular review of job content by a specialist.

6. *The number of industries in the corporation*

Even if a company seeks to follow a uniform pattern in wage matters, practices in different industries represented in the company may make modifications necessary among the different plants. In such circumstances, the level of decision making may be in the division, and the exceptional plant may be permitted considerable deviation from standard practice. To the extent that the head of operations in one industry not only knows that industry's situation best but also takes account of the situation of the company as a whole, his recommendation tends to be approved and thus to be the final decision.

7. *Management's tendency to seek a balance between centralization and decentralization*

While top management exercises its need for adequate control of wages and salaries in many ways, there appears to be an almost automatic maintenance of balance between centralization and decentralization in this area. For example, when no formal wage structure was reported, it was found that wage rates were likely to be set at plant level but to be reviewed in detail by the industrial relations staff or a chief executive. When an approved job evaluation plan was in effect, plant management and supervisors had greater freedom in making changes within established ranges without final review by headquarters. As one executive pointed out, the corporation's interest can be protected either through an approved system or through review.

VIII. EMPLOYEE SECURITY PROGRAMS

A. HEALTH AND SAFETY

1. *Policy formulation and decision*

THERE appears to have been little change in the functions of the medical and safety staffs at company headquarters during the past fifteen years. In some cases, these staffs develop standards that are expected to be followed by all units of operation, in others the standards are recommended, and in still others the corporate medical and safety directors act only as consultants to the plant managers and their medical and safety staffs. The particular aspects of the medical or safety programs that are determined at the corporation and at the plant level also vary among the companies.

Policy decisions for both health and safety are centered at the corporate or division level in the majority of the forty companies giving information in this area, but medical programs or standards are centralized to a greater extent than safety. However, other things than the highest level of policy making must be taken into account in evaluating the extent of centralization and decentralization of these functions.

The health and safety policies established for the corporation as a whole usually cover only a part of the total health and safety programs in the operating units. Some corporation medical policies may establish only the requirement of pre-employment physical examinations and minimum standards for medical staff and medical units. Other company-wide specifications may cover a much larger part of plant medical programs. However, some part of each plant's program is, in all cases, worked out by the local manager and medical staff in consultation with the plant industrial relations manager and corporation medical director.

A greater proportion of safety than medical matters were found to be determined at the plant level. In fact, decentralization is a stated policy for safety matters more often than for any one other industrial relations function. Nevertheless, the corporation safety committee or director (who may report to the industrial relations director, the head of the engineering department, or the vice president of manufacturing) frequently sets standards to which all plants are expected to conform. The director of safety or a safety committee often also initiates or must approve specific changes that involve large sums of money. The necessity of staff determination and implementation of policy and line acceptance of full responsibility for day-to-day enforcement are shown in the following typical statements:

Safety is of prime importance. So much so that the company policy, as stated in the words of the Vice President of Operations, is as follows:

1. "Safety comes first in our Company—not one pound of steel should be produced or shipped at the expense of a disabled employee.

2. "We have no place in our Company for supervisors who have no time for safety.

3. "Safety is not only the responsibility of the Safety Department, but it is the responsibility of everyone in the Company."

"The Management of the . . . Refinery accepts the responsibility for accident and fire prevention in accordance with the policy of the . . . Company and the Manufacturing Department; namely, to maintain an effective accident and fire prevention program in all operations, activities, procedures, and employee relations at all locations and under all conditions; further that executives, managers, superintendents, and foremen are responsible and charged with meeting their individual and collective responsibilities in connection with this policy as a vital and essential part of their duties, in proportion to their position or rank in the Company organization."

2. *Responsibility for application of health and safety policies*

An analysis of the highest point of responsibility for decisions on medical activities shows that among 30 companies, 21 delegate full responsibility for the application of health and sanitation policies to plant management; in nine, certain decisions may be referred to the division level or to the corporation medical director or head of manufacturing. The situation is similar for the application of safety policies. As in other functions, even though decision on application of policy rests with plant management, there may be, and usually is, frequent consultation between the special plant staff and its counterpart at headquarters.

For both health and safety matters, the determination of basic policy, and the day-to-day decisions relative to its application, coordination and control are interwoven and often difficult to distinguish. The following are typical company statements:

"Health and sanitation is the responsibility of the local plant management with advisory help from the Central Staff Plant Engineer and the Central Medical Department of the Corporation. Such questions are subjects for bargaining by the unions but are not arbitrable under the terms of current agreements.

"Safety is the responsibility of the local plant, administered through safety representatives who are responsible to the plant engineer. The Central Personnel Department has the responsibility of keeping corporate statistics on safety. Central Staff Plant Engineer has a safety man on his staff who holds regular meetings with plant safety personnel and gives such advice and consultation to local plants as may be requested."

"We have a corporate medical program covered by Code statement and a corporate plant sanitation program administered through our Manufacturing and Engineering Department. Not negotiated.

"We have a corporate safety program which is carried out by local units with guidance and control from Headquarters Training Division. Not negotiated."

The common pattern is for the medical and safety directors (or, for the latter function, a special committee) to set standards and to see that plant management maintains these standards. When the standards are being established in a new plant, or a new hazard is being studied, or a large sum of money may be involved, the top level staff is likely to share in or make decisions on application of policy. As standards are established and precedents set, the plant medical or safety staff is likely to be the highest point of referral with the day-to-day responsibility for sanitary and safe working conditions accepted as part of the supervisor's job.

3. Factors affecting the levels of responsibility for health and safety

There appears to be considerable relationship between the overall degree of centralization in a company and the level at which policy decisions for health and safety matters are made. Among the companies with a high degree of centralization, 77 per cent determine their medical policies, and 68 per cent safety policies, at the corporation or division level. In contrast, of the companies rated as being "balanced" between centralization and decentralization, only 31 per cent determine their health policies and 40 per cent their safety policies at the top level.

Size of company apparently is not a factor in the extent of centralization or decentralization of health or safety decisions. Size of plant was mentioned as a factor, but since bigness was mentioned as an influence both towards centralization and decentralization, it is evident that size of plant is incidental to other factors, especially to the degree of hazard involved.

The following are factors that appear to have the greatest influence on the level of decision making in the functions of health and safety:

(1) The extent of the risk of occupational disease or serious accident.

When the manufacturing processes carry considerable risk of industrial disease or accident, health and safety policies and close control of centrally established standards are inevitably the responsibility of a top level special staff or committee. However, centralization and decentralization go hand-in-hand since emphasis is also given to the continuous responsibility of all levels of management.

In one company, for example:

> The industry is hazardous with danger of lead poisoning and burns. Hence, extensive and costly medical departments are set up and safety measures taken. The development of policies and standards is the responsibility of the corporation industrial relations division. Line management administers the policies which are coordinated by the plant and division medical staffs and safety engineers. Safety courses for supervisors are set up with the help of the central staff only at the request of operating units.

(2) The specialized nature of the function.

The difference in the degree of centralization of health and safety matters is in part due to the difference in the professional or specialized nature of the two functions. Health problems cannot be solved without the help of a doctor, and the specialized knowledge of an experienced medical director is needed when planning a wide or a limited plant medical program. Companies, recognizing the importance of the competence of the individual doctor, often make the selection of plant medical directors or consultants dependent upon the approval of the corporation medical director or a higher officer. Safety engineering is also a specialization but one in which many members of management have had some training and experience. For this reason, safety is more easily integrated with general management, permitting the safety engineer to act in a distinctly advisory and control basis.

(3) Company philosophy with respect to the extent of medical care to be provided by an employer.

This factor seems to operate independently of the risk of disease or accident in the manufacturing processes. Companies of similar size and in the same industry may, on the one hand, provide a minimum of medical care administered primarily at the plant level, and, on the other, may encourage in all plants an extensive diagnostic service or program of medical care coordinated by the corporation medical officer. A recent development initiated and usually administered at the corporation level is a program of health examination for executives.

(4) The need for uniformity of reporting.

Uniform reporting of in-plant accidents and occupational disease is essential both as a legal matter and for purposes of a company's own control. Report forms are prepared by the corporation staff, and reports submitted to, and the data on them collated by, the same central staff. The requirement of periodic reports to the division or top staff is itself a not unimportant factor in the attention given to the particular function by the plant manager and his staff.

(5) Need for employee and union cooperation.

Companies recognize that a good accident record and sanitary working conditions require the cooperation of every employee. Unions are also interested in the health and safety of their members. The result of this common interest is that a clause on health and safety appears in most union contracts. When multiplant contracts are negotiated, such a clause is frequently in both the master contract and the supplementary plant contracts. The reference to safety and health in contracts at both levels emphasizes the corporation-wide responsibility for safety and health. The joint safety committees, whether or not mentioned in the agreement, give special emphasis to the interest of the employee in the working conditions immediately around him and tend to encourage the delegation of responsibility in the safety and health functions.

B. PENSIONS

1. *Policy formulation and decision*

In every one of the companies that gave information on procedures in pension planning, the formulation of a plan and decision as to the type of plan and the extent of its application were made at the corporation level. Certain influences have resulted, in a few cases, in the establishment of employee pension plans on less than a corporation-wide basis. However, final decision permitting establishment of a plan on a local basis or excluding certain groups of employees or certain plants from the corporation plan has been made by the board of directors or the executive committee. The principal corporation plan is also submitted to the vote of the stockholders.

Typical procedure, now as in the past, is formulation of a plan or revisions by the central industrial relations staff or a special committee with the help of pension consultants, discussion by the executive committee, approval of legal aspects, final approval by the board of directors, and submission to the stockholders. The most important influence for change in procedure is the requirement that companies bargain on pension plans. This factor has affected company procedures in several ways. Companies with multiplant contracts have generally negotiated a pension plan for the same area as the labor contract. Companies bargaining on a plant basis either have succeeded in maintaining the established uniform plan with or without union agreement, or have negotiated local modifications in the basic plan. Some reason, other than the union situation, was given by three companies for the establishment of an employee pension program on less than a corporation-wide basis.

The companies that have been able to maintain largely unilateral procedures in pension planning are of two sorts: (1) few of their plants are organized or the local unions do not have the strength to secure a plan or a change in plan; (2) the corporations' plants are organized by many different national unions or by unaffiliated locals, and the corporation pension plan is as generous or better than the types of plans the unions have succeeded in negotiating with other companies. An important factor in the company's ability to maintain unilateral control of pension planning appears to be not only the comparative generosity of its plans but the willingness to make company-initiated changes in accord with valid employee or union criticism of the plan. Keeping plans currently abreast of best pension practice requires the participation of all supervisors and plant managers in reporting criticisms of the pension plan. It is of interest that union criticism is an influence towards decentralization in this particular activity. For the effect of supervisory participation is, as was evident from interviews in several plants of one company, to enhance the supervisors' interest, to give them the feeling that the information they provide is really helpful to top management decision, and to make them more competent to answer employee and shop steward criticism of the pension plan.

A better understanding of pension problems among plant managerial personnel may also be the result of bargaining on a pension program at the local plants. The industrial relations manager of one company (whose bargaining on a local basis required the closest coordination between the central industrial relations department and the different plants) was confident that at the end of negotiations the plant managers knew more about the pension plan than ever before, and that supervisors, employees, and union leaders knew more fully how well the company's plan compared with others.

One company with a multiplant agreement in the plants of its primary industry and separate contracts for individual plants represented by a variety of unions reported:

> "We have negotiated *seven* pension plans. . . . We don't have them with all our unions. We negotiate at the separate plants [except for the plants in the one industry], but the broad limits are set by the Employee Welfare Board."

The introductory paragraph to one of the negotiated pension plans shows that the final decision on the part of this company is, as is true for all of the companies surveyed, even higher than the Welfare Board:

> "This Pension Agreement is contingent upon and subject to obtaining the approval of the stockholders of the Company, and is also contingent upon and subject to obtaining and retaining such approval of the Commissioner of Internal Revenue, as the Company in its sole discretion shall consider necessary. . . ."

The acceptance of non-uniform pension arrangements in this company may be due to the fact that employees, according to the indications of recent attitude surveys made for the company, tend to identify themselves with their plant and industry rather than with the corporation.

In another company in which two master contracts covering several plants each are signed with two different unions, and other contracts are negotiated plant by plant, the pension plans of the corporation have varied in provision and in time of installation both among the divisions of the corporation and within the principal division. The divisional personnel manager first reported that:

> "Over-all policies [for pensions] are determined by the [Division] Personnel Department and administered at that level. Subject to negotiation."

In a later interview, he indicated much greater centralization, stating that a retirement benefits committee had been set up at the central office "to look into this problem, to develop policy, and to make decisions in these matters." Most of the members of this committee are corporation directors.

One temporary influence against a company-wide, uniform pension plan reported by a few companies was the non-existence of any pension plan in recently purchased plants. When a new plant is far removed from the other plants of the company and its employees have not previously been covered by a retirement plan, companies tend to weigh carefully all the problems involved before extending the corporation plan to the new plant. One executive stated that his company would introduce its benefit plans into a new branch "only as time indicates its desirability."

2. *Responsibility for application of policy*

a. Typical procedure

Administration of pension programs, like decisions establishing them, is highly centralized. Procedures are established by the central pension or benefit board (or by the insurance carrier), routine announcements to individuals prior to retirement are sent either from the central board or from the plant personnel office, and pre-retirement discussion with the individual employee is with his supervisor or some member of the plant personnel staff or with both.

Action in exceptional cases (such as early or postponed retirement) may be initiated by the supervisor, the plant manager, or the plant personnel officer. Whoever initiates action, it must have the approval of the plant manager, perhaps also that of the head of the division, and always the final approval of the special board or administrative committee. For example, in one company, the plant manager initiates the request for deferred retirement, the head of the division involved recommends such deferment, and the recommendation is approved or rejected by the pension board. The same company has a plan of special benefits for annuitants whose pensions are inadequate. The plant personnel office plays a primary part in its administration, being responsible for an investigation of the individual's circumstances and for a report to the central board. However, the board makes the decision as to the amount of the supplementary payment.

b. New elements in pension administration and their effect on the level of decision making

Three recent developments have tended to spread the administration of pensions beyond its previous concentration in the local personnel office and the central pension board. These are: (1) union participation in administration; (2) pressures for greater flexibility in retirement age; and (3) increasing interest in pre-retirement counseling.

Some companies that have negotiated pension plans have maintained complete control of administration, some have agreed to permit disputes concerning certain aspects of administration to be taken to arbitration, and others have agreed to joint management-union boards of administration. None of the companies giving information on this subject had been forced by any appeal outside the company to submit to arbitration grievances arising out of the administration of the plan unless this had been agreed to in the contract.

One negotiated pension plan that established an administrative board made up wholly of management people specified that grievances on any of the following items could be referred "for final and binding decision to an arbitrator. . . ."

"(1) the number of years of continuous service of such applicant; or

(2) the age of such applicant; or

(3) whether an Employee retired on pension by the Company between the 65th and 68th anniversary of his birth is unable to perform satisfactorily work assigned to him or whether there is no available work to which he can be transferred and which he could perform satisfactorily; or

(4) whether an applicant for a pension on the ground of total and permanent disability under paragraph B of Section 1 of this Part I shall have become totally and permanently disabled by reason of unavoidable cause as defined in said paragraph B. . . ."

Another negotiated plan set up "a central Board of Administration . . . composed of six members, three appointed by the Corporation and three by the Union." It further provided that:

"As soon as possible after the effective date of this Agreement, the Union and Corporation members of the Board of Administration shall work out matters such as but not limited to: (1) procedures for establishing local pension committees at the Divisions or plants involved; (2) the authority and duties of such local pension committees; (3) the procedures for reviewing applications for pensions; (4) the handling of complaints regarding the determination of age, service credits, and computation of benefits; (5) procedures for making appeals to the Board; (6) means of verifying service credits to which employes are entitled under the Plan; (7) methods of furnishing information to employes regarding past and future service credits; (8) the amount of time the Union members of the local committees may be permitted to leave their work to attend meetings of the local pension committees; (9) how disputes over total and permanent disability claims will be handled; (10) the review of pertinent information about the Plan for dissemination to employes; (11) how pension payments will be authorized by the Board. . . ."

To the extent that retirement is discretionary beyond the normal retirement age and the company seeks to weed out the most inefficient workers among the past-65 group, the special pension administrators must look to supervisors for assistance. The responsibility for recommending retirement for individuals who cannot keep up with their work is one that, in the opinion of managements, supervisors prefer to avoid. However, if flexibility in retirement age becomes more common, the first line supervisor will be involved at least to the extent of referring problem cases to the personnel department.

A study made in 1952 of the retirement practices of 14 firms[1] revealed only one that was attempting to install pre-retirement counseling throughout the company. In others, the inauguration of such plans was dependent upon the interest of an individual plant manager or member of a plant personnel staff. Companies were willing to have individual units of the organization experiment with counseling, and to this extent were encouraging more interest among and granting more leeway to plant management on retirement procedures.

3. Factors affecting the continued high level of policy determination and application

Five factors appear to be of most importance in the continuing high degree of centralization of pension planning and administration in spite of the current developments, referred to above, creating some pressure towards decentralization. These factors are:

(1) the large sums of money involved
(2) the long-term and legal nature of commitments
(3) the need for the services of a specialist in formulating a plan or modifying one
(4) the desirability of wide coverage
(5) the desirability of uniformity

The size of expenditures involved and the long-term and contractual nature of commitments make pension planning a matter of concern for the highest level of management and even of the stockholders. Plant managers and division heads cannot be permitted to make decisions that may make the corporation as a whole responsible for payments to an individual that may be insignificant for one year but, in terms of a man's life expectancy, amount to more than any division or plant manager may authorize. For the same reason, action with respect to early retirement, supplementary benefits, and similar matters may be initiated by plant management, but final decision is reserved for a special board or committee responsible to the chief executive or board of directors.

The technicalities involved in pension planning require the services of outside consultants or a staff of specialists within the corporation. In either case, the costliness of advisory services is such that economy

---

[1] Baker, H. *Retirement procedures under compulsory and flexible retirement policies.* Industrial Relations Section, Princeton University. p. 48.

demands they be utilized on a centralized basis rather than by the individual plants.

Since the composition of the work force is an important factor in pension costs, companies are aware of the importance of wide coverage to assure a balanced composition of the total group covered by the pension program. A number of companies—all with less than 5,000 employees—reported problems arising as the result of company purchase of plants that had been in operation for many years but had made no arrangements for employee annuities. Some of these newly-acquired plants had a high percentage of older workers or of women, for whom pension costs would be high. The new owners had to choose one of several alternative courses of action. Whatever the decision, the composition of the local group was an important factor, but the decision invariably was made at the highest corporate level.

With the exception of temporary variations for newly acquired plants, companies generally agree on the desirability of equitable if not strictly uniform treatment of all employees on pension matters. Uniformity is especially important among supervisors and higher members of management who may be transferred from plant to plant or from plant to headquarters. This is one reason for the retention of a corporation-wide plan for salaried employees, even when the bargaining situation has forced a company to adopt more than one plan for its wage-earners. Those employers that want their employees and members of management alike to feel themselves a part of the corporation and that look upon their benefit programs as an important element in the individual's relationship to the corporation are most concerned with the maintenance of a uniform plan. Such companies are already facing the difficult question of whether it is more important to maintain local bargaining, even to the extent of modifications in the corporation's pension program, or to maintain a uniform pension plan at the cost of accepting limited multiplant bargaining.

C. Employee Savings and Company Profit-Sharing Plans

The determination of the level at which savings plans are established depends principally on the type of plan. Employee savings plans that involve no contribution by the company and a minimal expenditure for administrative assistance, on one hand, may be encouraged by the corporation, but decision as to their application within a particular plant rests with plant management. On the other hand, savings plans which include contributions by the company, either on a profit-sharing basis or as a percentage of employee contributions, invariably are established by action of the board of directors. Plans of the latter type are usually initiated and formulated by top management. However, decision as to participation in the plan and as to time and method of its introduction in the given division or plant may be at the discretion of the subsidiary or the division.

One corporation with an established savings program reported considerable variation among its subsidiaries. The corporation developed and gave necessary approval to aspects of the plan involving corporation funds. Most affiliates adopted the plan as recommended but added to or modified the plan according to conditions in the subsidiary. Thus, some contribute more and some less than was specified in the original plan. Two companies, which had established savings plans because local managements had reported interest in such a plan on the part of employees and of the union, had followed slightly different methods in installation. One company stated that:

> "Headquarters set up the principles governing the plan and 'bargained' with the union concerning them. (Labor contracts are negotiated on a local basis.) Little more could be done than to tell the union 'this is it.' It would have been impossible to have done otherwise, since there was no room for local discretion. Such items as administrative expense, company contribution, approval by the Bureau of Internal Revenue and the Wage Stabilization Board, and the filing of a registration statement with the Security Exchange Commission all had to be considered. The union also recognized these problems."

The other company, whose plan resulted from the report of some employee interest, also was formulated at the corporation level but was allowed to be adopted by affiliates as and when they saw fit. Since it was a generous plan, all but one affiliate followed suggested procedure and inaugurated the plan promptly. The one affiliate later "picked up and introduced the program as recommended by central management. However, this was on its own initiative."

The question of extending a generous pension and profit-sharing plan to recently purchased plants was referred to above. One company reporting this problem was of the opinion that, if acquired plants were to have pension plans, they would have to be established separately, since the affiliates now operate as separate entities for tax purposes.

It appears that the financial and technical factors influencing centralization of pension plans are similar to those to be taken into account in establishing an employee savings plan with company contributions. However, two other factors make the long-range, centralized planning problem much less compelling in relation to savings than in relation to pensions. A savings program is not considered by employees themselves as important to their security as a pension plan. There is comparatively little employee, union, or social pressure for the establishment of a savings or profit-sharing plan. (Only 20 out of 46 companies reported any kind of a savings plan.) A company may avoid the issue of decentralized bargaining *vs.* a centralized plan simply by failing to set up a plan. Also, since a company savings plan is not primarily associated with forced retirement, but, rather, usually permits an employee to use at least his own savings to meet current needs, a plan can be cancelled or modified or withheld from some divisions while offered to others without risking employee resentment.

D. Group Insurance and Sickness Benefits

1. *Policy decisions*

Some of the reasons for centralization of pension plans were also given as reasons for centralization of group insurance and sickness benefit programs. The fact that 88 per cent of the reporting companies required referral of decisions in insurance and benefits to top management as compared with 100 per cent of the companies requiring such referral for pensions indicates somewhat greater centralization than actually exists, especially for sickness benefits and hospitalization plans. The difference lies in the discretion in planning allowed to local managements.

As in pension planning, very little discretion is allowed to plant management on benefit programs when they have been, for a long time, an important part of the company's total employee relations program. In other cases, especially when companies have expanded by purchase of plants already in operation, or when they are dealing with a number of strong unions, local managements and unions may have considerable influence in retaining or adopting a plan not in accord with former company-wide policy. Such deviations, however, usually must have the approval of a special board or of the executive committee or board of directors.

Centralized decision making for insurance and benefit plans is of three general types: (1) the corporation initiates, formulates, adopts, and uses its influence to have all units accept an identical plan; (2) the corporation, on its own or the plants' initiative, studies the needs for a new plan or changes in a previous plan, recommends a certain plan or type of change, but allows variation among the plants according to local needs; (3) the plant may, with special assistance of the head-quarters industrial relations staff and subject to final approval by the board of directors of commitments for corporation expenditures, develop its own plan.

Because of the different problems connected with group life insurance, hospitalization and surgical benefit plans, and health insurance or sickness benefits, a given company may have a corporation-wide plan for, say, group life insurance and a variety of plans for sickness benefits or hospitalization. However, most of the companies reporting were in the first or second groups mentioned above. In only 11 per cent of the reporting companies was more than one of their several benefit plans largely formulated at the plant level.

One company with a long history of liberal benefit plans established on a central, uniform basis reported the following experience and procedures in connection with a recent change in its group life insurance plan:

> When a savings plan was being discussed, department general managers suggested that there was more immediate need for addition to the company's group life insurance program. Consequently the thrift plan was held up while a new contributory life insurance plan was studied by the central industrial relations department. The plan was discussed with department and plant managers and personnel staff, and was approved by the executive committee and the Board of Directors.
>
> Since it was a contributory plan, at least 75 per cent of those eligible had to participate if the plan were to go into effect; the central industrial relations department suggested, and the executive committee decided, that only employees with three years of service be eligible. When 87 per cent of those with three or more years of service elected to enter the plan, the departmental general managers wanted to lower the service requirement to one year. The industrial relations staff studied this possibility but decided that if the service requirement was thus reduced, participation would be too near the 75 per cent minimum required, and the staff convinced the general managers that it was preferable to maintain the three-year requirement for the time being.
>
> The company bargains on a local basis and union requests to bargain at a higher level have been referred back to the plants. It was assumed that union demands and employee opinions were reflected in line management suggestions. A clause negotiated for most of the local contracts is to the effect that as long as any plant in the company has a given program it will not be taken away from the plant represented by the union, and any change made for any other of the plants will be made for the one covered by the contract.
>
> In introducing the new program, printed material was used exten-

sively and meetings were held by the central industrial relations staff for local staff people who would handle the insurance program. Line supervisors handled the solicitation of employees to join the plan but have no responsibility for its administration.

While benefit plans in this company are centrally formulated and adopted by the board of directors with the expectation of their corporation-wide application, uniformity is gained through persuasion rather than through decree. However, failure to accede to persuasion was said to be rare. It also appeared from discussion with several plant managers that they were satisfied with the extent to which their ideas were solicited and deviation from common practice was permitted. These managers believed that, for such plans, a high degree of centralization was desirable.

Several companies with bargaining situations similar to the one just cited have uniformity in some but not all of their plans. In certain situations, variation has been accepted when local union demands coincided with other reasons for a different plan in one or more plants; in other cases, the parent company has established minimum standards for most of its benefit program and allowed plant managers to bargain locally on "such adaptations as were in keeping with local practice."

Companies with multiplant bargaining sometimes have retained what amounts to unilateral determination of benefit plans with limited variations in plans according to local need just as have companies with local bargaining. The extent to which this is possible appears to depend not only upon the bargaining strength of the union but also upon the liberality of the plan offered by management in comparison with what unions have won in other companies. When a company negotiates with a number of unions, the variety of union demands is a strong influence towards decentralization. Top management then is likely only to attempt to control the amount of the corporation's contribution but not the details of plans. The following report of one company is an example of different plans resulting from bargaining with many unions:

"Carrier [for group life insurance] usually determined by union, and company contributes to premium in accordance with labor agreement. Sickness and accident benefits bargained with local union and company selects insurance carrier and pays all or part of premium in accordance with labor agreement. For salaried personnel, local Blue Cross and Blue Shield. No sickness and accident benefits for salaried personnel because of liberal sick leave payments for salaried personnel. Policy in connection with such leaves determined by Employee Welfare Board."

2. *Responsibility for administration*

The administration of benefit programs varies from a high point of centralization for group life insurance to a high degree of decentralization for hospital insurance, sickness benefits, and leaves of absence. Death is a matter of record. Hospitalization and sickness benefits may require consultation by the local personnel staff or line supervisors with the employee and with the local hospital or the physician or surgeon in charge. When plans are established locally, the entire administration is local except for unusual cases which may set precedents or require expenditure of funds beyond the provision of the established plan. But even in company-wide hospital and sickness benefit plans, administration is largely the responsibility of plant management.

One company with a uniform sickness and accident disability plan including uniform procedures states that:

> "This Plan shall be administered, under the Direction of the Board of Directors, by local management and, subject only to questions of interpretation, local management may be given authority to decide conclusively all questions arising in administration."

In this case, "local management" refers to the supervisor responsible "for approving payment of time for the employee involved," and to the plant industrial relations office. The disabled employee must send the request-of-payment form to his supervisor.

> "Benefits will not be allowed by the supervisor until he has received the completed form and talked to the employee. . . . At the discretion of the supervisor, a physician's report may be required for absences of less than three days' duration. Upon completing his portion of the request form, the supervisor will forward the form to the Industrial Relations office for filing."

Another company with a company-wide "package plan" also emphasizes local administration. It stated, for instance:

> "All administration of hospitalization and sickness benefits is handled locally. The [local] industrial relations department follows up on hospitalization and doctors' bills to make sure that all final arrangements are taken care of and that the employee is not being overcharged."

Some companies with uniform plans put more emphasis on uniformity of administration. One industrial relations manual states:

> "While the responsibility for administering the Company's Plans and Practices is primarily a function of plant management, it is desirable that they be administered on a reasonably consistent basis Company-wide. The Industrial Relations Division . . . acts as a clearing house in this respect."

3. *Factors influencing the level of decision making*

Influences toward decision making at a high level for insurance and benefit plans are similar to those operating towards centralization of pension planning. However, the factors working towards decentralization are stronger for insurance and benefit plans than for pension matters. This is especially true of administrative decisions.

The principal factors favoring centralization are: (1) the sums of money involved and moral if not legal long-term commitments; (2) the need for the services of a specialist; (3) the desirability of wide coverage; and (4) desirability of uniformity.

Usually insurance and benefit plans are "term," and legally may be changed at the discretion of management or with a change in labor contract. However, as companies have discovered, it is difficult to withdraw benefits once established. As a result, management, in considering the costs of a new benefit plan, knows that it is establishing expectancies which not only may need to be met indefinitely but which may also be the basis for increased costs in the future.

The possible variations in benefits are numerous, and most companies want to know that they are getting the best combination of benefits purchasable by a specified sum or percentage of payroll. An expert's services are needed and are most economical when used at the top level of management decision. The fact that the costs of group life and health insurance are lower and more stable when the group covered is large gives a financial advantage to company-wide plans.[1]

The reporting companies that have emphasized their pension and benefit plans for many years are convinced that a uniform plan with as nearly uniform administration as is possible is an important element in good employee relations. However, companies that have established benefit plans more recently—either unilaterally or negotiated—seem to be less concerned with uniformity.

These influences towards centralization generally were thought to be of lesser importance in insurance and benefits than in pensions. The following factors appear to be the principal reasons for the less compelling nature of centralization in insurance and benefit plans: (1) variation in bargaining situations; (2) variation in local plant situation; (3) the importance of personal contacts and of a decision related to the individual's need.

Many companies have no choice but to bargain over benefits with

[1] Slavick, Fred. *The operation of sickness benefit plans in collective bargaining.* Princeton University. Industrial Relations Section. 1951. pp. 93-94.

more than one union. Where one predominant union among the company's plants or a coalition of unions would permit bargaining for one plan, many companies have chosen non-uniformity rather than multi-plant bargaining.

Even when collective bargaining is not an influence towards the local determination of plans, a different community situation, an established plan in a recently purchased plant, or state legislation may make it impractical to extend the corporation's program to a given plant or plants. One company, for example, has the Blue Cross hospitalization plan in all of its plants except one which is located where the hospitals do not cooperate in Blue Cross arrangements. A number commented that, if they were to insist on combining several local plans into a corporation-wide plan, they would have to incorporate the most liberal provisions of all the plans—a costly step.

The administration of sickness benefit programs is, in contrast to group life insurance, largely the responsibility of plant supervisors. The supervisor-employee relationship is emphasized to give the ill worker a sense of friendly contact with his workshop as well as to discourage malingering. The local industrial relations staff, however, almost invariably coordinates this supervisory activity according to specific, centrally established procedures which may head up to the corporation level. Centralization is needed to assure a complete record of company experience and to keep interpretations and costs reasonably in line.

These variable influences toward centralization and decentralization in insurance and benefit plans point up the dilemma resulting from the desire for both uniformity or consistency of treatment on the one hand, and application of a policy according to individual need, on the other. The latter is especially important in connection with sickness benefits and flexible retirement plans. Many companies attempt to resolve the dilemma by maintaining a uniform plan but delegating, within prescribed limits, decisions on individual cases. Such delegation to plant supervisors appears to be much more successful in connection with sickness benefits than in connection with flexible retirement. Approving temporary absences on a doctor's certification is a much more routine matter than appraising and reporting declining efficiency that may result in a worker's permanent separation from his job. The seriousness of the decision for the corporation and for the employee is, it is evident, a factor not only in top management's willingness to delegate but also in the willingness of members of lower levels to accept responsibility.

IX. LOCATION OF RESPONSIBILITY
FOR MANAGEMENT-UNION RELATIONS

AS a major aspect of industrial relations, collective bargaining, including the level at which negotiations are conducted, the area of bargaining, the status of the negotiators, and the modes of influence and control which plant and central management exercise in the negotiating process, must be taken into full account in considering the existing degree of centralization and decentralization. The responsibility for bargaining involves a complex of formalized procedures and informal relationships among plant and headquarters personnel. Only by considering all of these procedures and relationships can a reasonably accurate impression of the existing degree of centralization and decentralization of collective bargaining in multiplant companies be obtained.

A. The Unit of Bargaining

The 46 companies which were interviewed for this study were classified according to the exclusive or principal type of bargaining unit covering the majority of their unionized employees. The results are given in Table 8. It is of interest also that, while all of the 46 companies have

TABLE 8. UNIT OF BARGAINING FOR MAJORITY OF EMPLOYEES
IN 46 MULTIPLANT COMPANIES

Unit of bargaining	No. of cos.	% of total
Exclusively single plant	19 }	
Primarily single plant	8 }	59
Exclusively multiplant	0 }	
Primarily multiplant	17 }	37
Approximately evenly divided	2	4
Total	46	100

had experience with single-plant bargaining and that none is currently bargaining on an exclusively multiplant basis, almost 59 per cent bargain on both bases. Consequently, a majority of the cooperating companies were in a position to compare experience under the two systems.

B. Management Practices and Objectives in the Assignment of Responsibility for Management-Union Relations

1. *Negotiating at the plant level*

a. Responsibility for negotiation

Forty-four of the 46 companies supplied detailed information on the question as to what extent and by what means central management participated in the negotiation of single plant agreements. Their responses were then analyzed according to four types of participation listed in Table 9.

TABLE 9. HEADQUARTERS PARTICIPATION OR INFLUENCE
ON SINGLE PLANT NEGOTIATIONS IN 44 COMPANIES

Type of headquarters participation or influence	*No. of cos. mentioning each type of participation or influence*
(1) Membership on plant negotiating team	26
(2) Participation in the formulation of proposals	11
(3) Consultation between plant and headquarters	24
(4) Review and approval of contract	23

None of the 44 companies failed to exert some degree of centralized influence on the single plant negotiations, and many of them were found to use more than one method to influence the outcome of negotiations. In 60 per cent of these companies, someone from the head office participates in negotiations. Only 5 companies limit the means of headquarters' influence to review and approval. For the others, expediency is the general rule and the extent of headquarters participation varies according to circumstance. The only common feature that can be ascribed to all the categories of headquarters' influence in single plant negotiations is that all of them represent a mechanism intended to increase the possibility of attaining commonly desired results throughout the corporation.

(1) *Membership of headquarters personnel on plant negotiating team*

Twenty-six companies stated that someone from headquarters always, or as needed, participated directly in local negotiations. The participant, in 85 per cent of the companies was reported to be a member of the headquarters industrial relations staff. Other representatives mentioned were high level line executives, such as vice president of manufacturing.

The two principal roles played by headquarters' personnel at plant negotiations are that of "negotiator" and "advisor," although there are numerous variations in each of these. In 20 of the 26 companies, the headquarters' representative usually or frequently is the spokesman for management. Only six companies indicated that he is expected to act primarily in an advisory capacity. The following statement by a chief industrial relations executive suggests, however, the variation in role according to circumstance that is typical of many companies.

> The headquarters staff works constantly with local managements on labor matters. A representative of the headquarters department actually conducts negotiations in many locations. Our policy has been to develop the local management to the point where they are competent to handle negotiations directly though keeping in close touch with the headquarters staff on all developments and possible changes in union agreement. However, this is a slow development and a representative from our group still participates in person in about 50 per cent of the negotiations.

A company which sends a headquarters representative to plant negotiations under any and all circumstances is obviously more centralized than one which sends a representative only when requested by the plant manager. Some of the more general statements made were in terms of "usually, not always," "sometimes," "when requested," "when headquarters and plant officials consider it advisable." Most companies said that central management's participation in single plant negotiations depended upon one or another of the following specific circumstances: (a) the importance or newness of the bargaining issue or bargaining unit; (b) the ability and willingness of plant management to negotiate; (c) the union involved and the plant and company relationship with it; (d) the difficulty of negotiations.

(2) Headquarters' participation in the formulation of contract proposals

Several of the 26 companies which reported headquarters' participation in negotiations, also reported pre-negotiation conferences to determine the bargaining position which plant managements were to take. In three companies, headquarters' influence was limited to participation in the formulation of contract proposals. This procedure is distinguished from such other modes of influence as consultation, approval, and review in that it precedes or takes place at the same time as negotiations and that it involves a relatively formal establishment of bargaining limits and positions. Several companies reported the practice of holding a pre-negotiations conference attended by all the plant negotiators and the corporation director of industrial relations. In other companies, headquarters might participate only in the formulation of proposals dealing with important financial items, such as wage increases and benefit plans.

(3) Plant consultation with headquarters before and during negotiations

Ten companies reported that plants, when necessary, consult with headquarters during negotiations even though headquarters participates neither in the formulation of proposals nor in actual negotiations. The degree of influence exerted through "consultation" was difficult to determine. However, it appears that in the simplest situations only information on what other plants are doing is involved; in other situations, advice, including recommended limits, is given. That the terms "information" and "advice" do not adequately explain the phenomena of "consultation," "guidance and counsel," "maintaining close contact," and similar expressions was evidenced by some of the explanatory statements made. One company expected a plant to "fall in line" when—on the basis of information supplied it from headquarters—it saw that it was "out of line" with the others. Such factors as the point of initiation of consultation, the frequency of consultation, and the status and personalities of the individuals involved must be considered. Knowing when it is necessary to consult and knowing how to adjourn a negotiations session for the purpose of "thinking things over" are considered essential management skills.

(4) Headquarters review and approval of contract

The minimum central influence exerted in the case of single plant bargaining was review of the contract. As was seen in Table 9[1] approximately one-half of 44 companies require such a review; many of these same companies also reported practices involving more control. Returns from the survey of 89 companies (in which a question as to the requirement of headquarters review of labor contracts was the only one related to collective bargaining) revealed a much higher percentage reporting that a review of labor agreements was "used as a means of

[1] p. 151.

maintaining desired standards in industrial relations." Of the 89 companies, 80 require headquarters review of labor contracts, four have no labor agreements, and five gave no information.

The principal purposes of headquarters review mentioned were to look for controversial questions, changes that affect major company policy, and changes that have an impact on other plants of the company. In some cases, the review is made by the legal department for the purpose of eliminating ambiguous language and other legal flaws. Only a few companies reported a review by anyone outside the central industrial relations staff or legal department. One company requires single plant contracts to be approved by a corporation officer. In another company, the board of directors of the subsidiary reviews the contract. Review and approval usually take place as negotiations progress or just before the contract is signed. A few companies, however, review agreements after they have been signed. Such reviews, intended primarily to keep headquarters informed, exert a minimum of influence, helping only to avoid undesirable clauses in future contracts.

b. Reasons for favoring single plant bargaining

(1) *Local differences.* One of the most obvious and frequently mentioned factors making companies favor local bargaining was the fact that conditions in the various plants and in the communities differ. The following were reported to be influences towards bargaining on a local basis: (a) product and occupational differences; (b) local union differences; and (c) geographical differences. Aside from the geographical differences in wages, differences in community conditions and practices were thought to be important. These included different local holidays, different costs of living, varying degrees of industrialization, regional differences in the age and composition of the work force, different employment opportunities, and varying degrees of unionization. Sometimes local unions affiliated with the same international give greater emphasis to local differences when bargaining on a single plant as compared with a regional or multiplant basis. When the local unions of a given company represent many international unions and none of them predominates, agreements are almost always on a plant basis. When manufacturing processes have resulted in different industrial relations problems or have facilitated the organization of different plants by different unions, they also have been a factor strengthening bargaining at the local level.

(2) *Management attitude towards unions.* While management officers generally agreed that company bargaining power was greatest with

single plant contracts, they did not often emphasize this factor. Most of the references to it were made indirectly in such terms as: (a) an uncompromising opposition to company-wide bargaining; (b) a desire to prevent company-wide or industry-wide strikes; (c) a desire to increase the common interests of local union and plant. Some companies believe that the local unions are most representative of their employees, facilitate a higher degree of cooperation, and become more mature in collective bargaining when they are responsible for negotiating an agreement.

(3) *Fear of local resentment of outsiders.* Some company people felt that local managements, local unions, and employees were inclined to resent top management handling of negotiations on either a single or multiplant basis.

(4) *Ease of negotiations.* A few companies felt a need to allow plant personnel to conduct negotiations because headquarters found it difficult to handle all the negotiations.

(5) *Improvement of day-to-day relations.* It is felt that employees have more respect for the plant manager, and that the plant manager is more interested in good industrial relations when he does the negotiating.

c. Problems of single plant bargaining

Four principal problems that accompanied or made single plant bargaining difficult were mentioned by reporting companies. These were: (1) the possibility of whipsawing, (2) an unstable union political situation, (3) the often inferior bargaining ability of plant managers, and (4) the considerable difficulty of company-wide coordination of a multitude of locally negotiated contracts.

The disadvantage of single plant bargaining stated most frequently by company executives was whipsawing. This was referred to with varying degrees of concern or confidence. Some officials considered whipsawing inevitable and had had devastating experiences with it; others anticipated such action but had not yet encountered serious trouble; still others felt confident that they could counteract it. The companies that mentioned the possibility of greater political instability on the local level tended to minimize the importance of this factor. Contrary to the frequently encountered opinion that the bargaining power of the company is stronger under single plant bargaining, a few executives saw in single plant bargaining a loss of company bargaining power. In their opinion, an imbalance of economic strength and negotiating ability result when an "autonomus" plant has to bargain with negotiators from a large and powerful national union. Balancing local needs with company-wide policies is also felt by some to be more difficult when many plant managers negotiate separate contracts than when one contract is negotiated by the corporation industrial relations staff with the advice of plant managers.

In spite of these recognized difficulties, none of the companies with single plant bargaining felt them to be as serious as the problems that might accompany multiplant bargaining.

2. Multiplant bargaining

Twenty-two of the 46 companies interviewed gave detailed information on multiplant bargaining. In only 17 of these, however, was this type of bargaining predominant.

a. Responsibility for negotiation

Management's chief negotiator for a multiplant contract was found, invariably, to be someone from headquarters. In the majority of cases, the corporation industrial relations or labor relations manager or some other member of the staff is the chief negotiator. Executive vice presidents handle negotiations in a few of the reporting companies and plant managers and the industrial relations manager take turns in the leading role in one company.

Just as headquarters is frequently represented in the plant bargaining group, so the individual plants may be represented in multiplant bargaining. In 19 of the 22 companies, plant managers or other line supervisors are members of the bargaining committee. Only one company reported that plant managers sometimes handle negotiations for the basic contract. In other companies, their role is more limited, sometimes being no more than that of an observer. The few companies that reported no arrangement for plant personnel to participate in or observe negotiations stated that plant managers and supervisors were asked, well in advance of negotiations, for suggestions to be considered in the formulation of contract proposals. The division was in no case reported to have chief responsibility for multiplant negotiations, although divisional industrial relations managers participate in two companies and a division general manager in one.

The most commonly reported organization for negotiation is a management committee of which the chief negotiator is chairman and the plant managers, plant industrial relations managers, and (in a few cases) divisional personnel are members. Most companies, when referring to the role played by plant management, stated that plant representatives served in an advisory capacity with respect to "technical factors" or matters which referred specifically to a particular plant or plants.

A number of executives commented that the nature of bargaining requires that various plant points of view be consolidated into one company position. One industrial relations manager said that in a recent situation he had had to "ram" a standard for a particular job specification "down some plant managements' throats" since that was the only way to secure agreement on one standard. In one company in which plant managers are permitted to enter the discussion by addressing the co-chairman, pre-negotiation conferences assure that nothing will be said to hurt the company's bargaining position. Exceptional authority is given the plant representatives in the two companies in which a majority vote of plant managers determines the corporation position on controversial issues.

The greater responsibility of plant managers in multiplant bargaining is in negotiating the supplementary agreement for the individual plant. Having participated to some degree in the negotiation of the basic agreement, the plant management is informed both on the framework within which he must bargain with the local union and on union and management attitudes. One company, to prevent the basic negotiations from being concerned with local questions, requires all local issues to be settled prior to the multiplant bargaining. Whatever the procedure, most companies continue to review supplementary contracts in order to be kept informed and to make sure there is no conflict between the basic and supplementary agreements.

b. Reasons for favoring multiplant bargaining

Four principal reasons for multiplant bargaining were mentioned by the 17 companies whose bargaining is primarily of this type. The reasons are: (1) the avoidance of whipsawing tactics; (2) the greater responsibility of the international unions and a strengthening of their control over local unions; (3) the better handling of company-wide activities; and (4) the greater efficiency of negotiations and administration of the agreement.

A frequently mentioned weakness of single plant bargaining was the danger of whipsawing. A number of executives said, in effect, that multiplant bargaining was better than "simultaneous attacks by a strong union at several points." Others had found that the international officers were generally more responsible than local officers and that they could exercise this responsibility best when they bargained simultaneously for all of the locals representing the employees of a given company. However, one company felt that this hoped for development had not occurred because of the political strength of a few locals. There was considerable agreement, even among companies which favored single plant contracts, that some matters are best handled on a centralized basis. Most companies also agreed that multiplant bargaining permitted the best use of skilled negotiators and legal talent.

c. Problems in multiplant bargaining

Many of the companies with multiplant contracts recognized difficulties pointed out by companies that were "holding the line" on single plant bargaining. They realized that special precautions had to be taken to avoid increasing the gap between management and workers, inadequate consideration of local conditions, and local resentment against a contract imposed upon them. There was a general feeling, however, that these weaknesses do not necessarily follow multiplant bargaining. They can be avoided if the chief negotiator consults with plant managers prior to negotiations and brings them into negotiations in every possible way, and if the division of responsibility for the application of the contract is clearly defined. If this effort is made, in the opinion of some executives, plant managers may be happier and more interested in industrial relations than when they themselves have the difficult task of negotiating a local contract acceptable both to top management and the national union.

Certain other problems pointed out in multiplant bargaining cannot be solved by plant participation. These were a worsening of competitive disadvantage with respect to companies having no unions, and the possible increase in the bargaining power of the union. Some companies have avoided the former problem by making base rates a part of local bargaining. A number of companies also felt that the question of relative bargaining strength could be argued both ways, and that a strong union had to be met by strong company negotiators whether on a local or multiplant basis.

It is evident that multiplant bargaining can be an influence towards centralization. But even with single plant bargaining, both top management's and the international union's vital interest in the labor contract are also centralizing influences. To what extent multiplant bargaining is a stronger influence in this direction than local bargaining controlled from company and union headquarters is difficult to assess.

Companies with multiplant contracts apparently can maintain a policy of delegation of responsibility comparable to that under single plant bargaining. However, more effort may be required to secure this result where multiplant contracts exist. An informal aid to decentralization is collusion by local union and local management against contracts or rules established by corporation and national union. This phenomenon seems to occur under both single and multiplant contracts, but was reported more often as a weakness accompanying supplements to multiplant contracts. The increasing emphasis on delegation of responsibility for labor relations in a few companies seemed to be motivated partly by a desire to avoid such informal and sometimes troublesome decentralization by placing more responsibility and accountability on the plant manager.

3. *The settlement of grievances and decision to arbitrate*

a. Formal location of responsibility

Formal grievance and arbitration procedures are established by the labor contract; their determination is the responsibility of those who negotiate and approve the contract. As has been shown, both activities involve a high degree of centralization. In contrast, managements continually stated that the application of the contract was almost wholly the responsibility of plant management. Disciplinary action and the settlement of grievances were considered primary responsibilities of the foremen.

An analysis of information received sought to find out: (1) the highest levels to which grievances can be referred under formal procedures; (2) the difference, if any, in this respect between companies bargaining primarily on a multiplant basis and those bargaining on a single plant basis; and (3) the effective level of decision making as seen in the informal handling of grievances.

The last step in the formal grievance procedure among the reporting companies ranged from the plant industrial relations manager to a chief officer of the corporation. Two-thirds of the companies bargaining primarily on a multiplant basis permitted appeal to the corporation level, as compared with less than one-third of those bargaining primarily or exclusively on a single plant basis. Formal or informal participation of a corporate officer or staff member in a decision to appeal to arbitration was reported by nearly 80 per cent of the companies bargaining on a multiplant basis as compared with slightly more than 60 per cent of the companies bargaining primarily or exclusively on a plant basis.

Another finding was that the plant or corporation industrial relations director represented the final step in the grievance procedure almost twice as often among companies bargaining primarily on a multiplant basis as among those with primarily single plant bargaining. The established procedure within a given company was found sometimes to vary between single and multiplant contracts and sometimes to be the same in both types of contract.

b. Informal procedures

The practice of informal consultation with headquarters appears to be much more common than formal procedures indicate. Whenever a specific case has implications for more than one plant, the corporation is likely to be interested in determining whether or not it is the best case and the best time to submit to arbitration. Information given headquarters early in the grievance procedure permits the central industrial relations staff of many companies to help their plants avoid getting into an "awkward" position. After one or two unfavorable decisions against a plant, few companies are willing to let the plant manager refer cases to arbitration without prior review of the situation by the central industrial relations department.

The comments of foremen in various plants and their description of the way they handle a disciplinary problem or an employee complaint revealed the extent to which these matters are discussed at higher levels, even when decision is nominally made by the foreman. The most common practice found was: the foreman discusses the problem with the general foreman or department head, who, depending on the uniqueness or significance of the problem, may or may not discuss it with the plant personnel manager, who, in turn, may discuss it with the headquarters staff. The foreman may suggest how he would like to handle the complaint or may recommend disciplinary action. While it is nearly always the foreman's responsibility to "hand out" the decision, the decision is rarely made by him alone.

A detailed comparison of formal and informal procedures in a plant of 600 employees operating under a single contract with procedures in a slightly larger plant operating under a master contract revealed almost identical formal procedures, similar favorable management attitudes towards delegation, and similar satisfactory results with informal procedures. Since the two plants were parts of two companies with very different bargaining experience, it was surprising to find so many similarities in management attitudes and procedures, and in the small number of grievances carried as high as the second or third steps.

Both plant managers were of the opinion that too many of their foremen were afraid to settle grievances on their own, but both also said they encouraged foremen to discuss with a higher authority any question that was unique or might affect other departments of the plant. The foremen themselves in the single plant bargaining situation as well as those in the plant operating under a basic contract pointed out the need to refer important questions to the industrial relations department for two reasons: (1) the industrial relations department has the records and can review the single complaint or disciplinary problem in the light of the man's full personnel record as well as other grievance settlements; and (2) the industrial relations manager is in the best position to weigh the effect of a given decision on the plant as a whole and its possible impact on other plants.

The chief difference in the two situations was that the foremen working with the single plant contract made no mention of their fear of reversal of a decision (although the plant manager and industrial relations manager believed this fear existed). In the second plant, several foremen expressed such a fear and blamed it on management's "catering to the union." They said "You have to work with the shop steward to settle grievances," or "If the union puts up a real fight, I don't press the matter, since management is likely to support the union anyhow." In this plant, operating under a master contract, the local union said they discussed important questions with the foreman only because plant management insisted on this formality. "We know that anything of importance is referred to the department superintendent or industrial relations manager." The local union in the first situation was of the opinion that foremen could handle grievances in a few departments but not in most. The difference, according to the union, depended on the attitude of the department head towards the union and his willingness to delegate.

These two small plants may not be typical of large plants with a greater ratio of workers to foremen and conditions less encouraging to informal relationships. The following reports are probably more typical of such companies: An executive of one very large company which bargains on a multiplant basis, and in which the final step in the grievance procedure is at the corporation level and unsettled grievances are referred to a permanent impartial umpire, commented that the existence of a permanent arbitrator might be one reason for the frequent appeals to arbitration. Another company with multiplant contracts reported considerable success in a definite drive to push grievances back to the plant. Interviews at one of its plants indicated that success in this drive had not yet reached lower levels, since a majority of formal grievances were still referred to the plant personnel manager. It was his opinion that it would take a long time to educate foremen to accept more responsibility of this nature.

Both large and smaller companies referred to a major problem: how to delegate responsibility for industrial relations to the foremen and give them greater competency in this responsibility, and at the same time avoid the risk of inconsistent decisions and the resulting need for reversal. This problem is made more difficult by a tendency of the union to by-pass the foreman and go directly to those who advise him and can make a decision that "will stick."

Informal consultation seems to be the frequent means of working out a practicable compromise. It is "face-saving" and, if the person consulted is a good teacher, it may help to develop the foreman's ability and self-confidence. Foreman discussion with higher management and with the shop steward prior to disciplinary action helps avoid the start of a grievance, and discussion of less serious complaints keeps them from being built up into formal grievances. The prompt and satisfactory settlement of minor grievances by means of informal procedures appears to depend upon several conditions: (1) the foreman's acceptance of the need to consult; (2) his department head's skill in helping the foreman and in giving him credit for a joint decision; (3) friendly personal relationships between foreman and his superior and with the union; and (4) the plant manager's and industrial relations manager's real desire to have most grievances settled informally by each department. Relationships and attitudes, it is evident, are more important in the satisfactory settlement of grievances than who actually makes the decision.

C. Union Attitudes Toward Management Goals and Practices with Respect to the Level of Bargaining and the Application of the Contract

What do unions think of management decentralization? Only 4 out of the 17 unions interviewed believed that the managements they dealt with operated on a decentralized basis in their labor relations. On the contrary, a number of comments were to the effect that the union had to deal with a "tight, monolithic organization" where "the reins of power are held by the central industrial relations office."

In the opinion of many union leaders, the power of the industrial relations staff, at both the headquarters and plant level, is constantly growing at the expense of the authority of the plant manager and others in the line organization, particularly the foreman. Other union officers thought that companies found it to their advantage to keep the "myth

of decentralization" alive "because an impression of too much centralized control would make them too vulnerable under the anti-trust laws."
Interestingly, some unions opposed local bargaining arrangements on
the same grounds as management—that it could be used as a means of
whipsawing. Even those unions which acknowledged a degree of decentralization in some of the companies they dealt with thought that limits
were set by headquarters for many items negotiated locally. In short,
most union officials were not convinced of the fact of decentralization,
and were, in some cases, suspicious of the motives of decentralization.

1. *Union opinion concerning the authority of the plant manager in labor relations*

Companies that prefer decentralized operations sometimes refer to
their plant managers as people who act "as if they were running their
own business." As seen by some union leaders, however, plant managers "can't move before getting instructions from headquarters," or
they act "like automatons" in local bargaining. The research director
of one union reported a situation where headquarters officials would
refuse to talk to an international union officer because it was claimed
that the issues involved were locally determined. Plant management,
on the other hand, insisted that it had no authority and could not act
without head office decision.

In the experience of one union dealing primarily with single plant
agreements, hardly any plant manager was free to settle a contract.
Another union, dealing primarily in multiplant and multi-company
agreements, found that plant managers had to check with corporate
industrial relations headquarters more under company-wide bargaining
than they previously did under single plant bargaining. An officer of a
third union felt that an increase in the number of cases taken to arbitration in a few large companies was primarily the result of the decreased authority of plant managers. Only a few unions were convinced
that some of the companies they dealt with really tried to give their
plant managers a noticeable degree of independence in handling their
employee relations. These unions also favored more independence for
their local officers. They contended, however, that the trend is toward
centralization and cannot be reversed. Such factors as size, the use of
special techniques, and labor legislation require special staffs on both
sides. Special staffs, according to this opinion, are the heart of centralization and neither the large company nor the large union can get along
without them.

2. *Opinion concerning the authority of the foreman*

There was almost unanimous agreement among those union leaders who expressed themselves on the subject that the authority of the foreman was exceedingly small. Even in those cases where union officials encouraged their membership to consult foremen first on day-to-day problems, such responses as these were heard: "Union stewards claim that foremen cannot settle grievances"; and, in direct contrast with the foremen statements with respect to grievances, "95 per cent of all but very minor cases are settled by the plant personnel manager or his assistant." Other unions complained that every important grievance had to be cleared through the central office, or that "the foremen's role now has become formalized and set up in a series of handbook instructions."

To what did unions ascribe this lack of authority? Some thought that higher supervision didn't know how to delegate or that management did not have confidence in the foremen's judgment and did not consider them technically competent to assume greater responsibility. A few unions thought that companies feared union whipsawing tactics; and one accused management of deliberately allowing grievances to reach the arbitration stage in order to burden the union treasury with the high cost of arbitration. In addition to such general criticism of management, plant personnel managers were a particular union target. Several unions attributed the decline of the foreman's authority to the advent of the plant personnel manager who, in order to obtain an ever larger budget, likes to inflate his importance. However, foremen themselves were also criticized for their unwillingness to assume responsibility (a criticism with which a substantial number of management people agreed).

3. *The basis of union attitudes*

Union criticism of managements' stated goals for decentralization appears to be, in part, an appraisal of the lack of plant autonomy and of limitations on lower supervision's authority in labor relations and, in part, an expression of the national unions' preference for multiplant or company-wide bargaining.

Two to three times as many unions preferred company-wide or industry-wide bargaining as favored single plant bargaining. Almost all of the unions preferred some degree of uniformity in their contracts. This predominant preference for uniformity and a broader unit of bargaining is not surprising since one of the basic tenets of labor organizations is that labor should not be a basis of competition. However, preferences usually were explained by more immediate considerations.

The unions interviewed generally agreed with management that multiplant or multi-company bargaining tended to increase union strength as compared with that of the companies involved. Statements like the following were made: "The stronger locals are really not being held back very much by multiplant bargaining, whereas the weaker locals are being helped quite a bit"; "generally speaking, unions tend to gain more from central agreements and companies from local ones"; and, "in terms of economic gains, more is gained by less effort in multiplant bargaining." A number of union officers, like some company executives, thought that central bargaining would improve overall union-management relations because of the greater contact between the responsible parties and because professionals would be dealing with problems in a more rational manner.

A few union officers agreed with management executives on certain other criticisms of multiplant bargaining: that adjustment to local needs sometimes suffers under multiplant bargaining; that some local unions, just as local managements, may disagree with the majority on important issues but be forced to accept uniform treatment. Strong local unions had a particular complaint in that they felt that they could do better if they bargained alone.

Union officers disagreed among themselves as to the effect of multiplant agreements on local leadership. Some thought that shop stewards and foremen had less and less authority because the locus of decision making tended to be higher. Other union officers believed that a large enough area for local initiative remained in the day-to-day handling of grievances and in the formulation and application of seniority rules.

The frequent statement by local unions that they prefer their shop stewards to settle grievances in the shop if the foremen have authority to settle reflected both an uneasiness with union centralization and strong criticism of intra-management informal consultation from which the union was excluded. Criticism was less when the union was a party to the informal discussion. Some unions recognized the inadequacy of the shop stewards as well as of the foremen, but these also felt that "behind-the-scenes" consultation excluding union representatives did nothing to improve the situation. The problems in delegation common to management and the union were rarely mentioned by unions critical of management's lack of effective decentralization.

D. Factors in the Location of Responsibility for Collective Bargaining

Cause and effect in the area here concerned are often too closely related to be distinguished easily. This is particularly true of the level of responsibility for bargaining and the area of bargaining. Multiplant bargaining is sometimes blamed for increased centralization. The findings of this study lend some support to this thesis. They also show, however, that centralized decision making in a company often precedes multi-unit bargaining, and that the centralizing effect of a multiplant contract can be avoided or kept to a minimum if a company makes a strong effort to do so. It was found, also, that single plant bargaining did not insure decentralization since local contracts negotiated by or under the close supervision of representatives of a single top management and a single international union might result in as much uniformity as a company-wide contract.

The following four groups of factors appear to be the principal determinants of the level at which company responsibility for labor relations rests—whether the company conducts its bargaining primarily on a single plant or on a multiplant basis. However, these factors are interacting and variable. Even within one large company, not only may both single and multiplant bargaining exist but the actual degree of centralization in decisions related to bargaining may vary from time to time. Sound decisions and successful bargaining seem to result more from flexibility to varying circumstance than to rigid adherence to certain procedures in either multiplant or single plant bargaining.

1. Conditions of management

a. Management's past and present attitude towards centralization and decentralization is an important factor in assuring any substantial degree of authority and participation to the plant managers under either multiplant or single plant contracts. A change from a philosophy of centralization to one of decentralization takes a long time to seep down to lower levels of supervision. If a foreman has had "his fingers burnt" even once, that experience influences his willingness to make or not make a decision on his own more than any number of exhortations to use his own best judgment. Effective handling of informal referrals is essential both to avoid reversals and to rebuild the foreman's self-confidence once he has had a decision formally reversed.

b. Companies that want bargaining to be handled locally by local management make a special effort to develop skilled negotiators in the plants. The labor contract in any plant is of such importance to the company as a whole that, if a plant manager or plant industrial relations manager cannot handle negotiations, someone from headquarters will take over the bargaining. Bargaining skill requires both competency in meeting the union representatives and the ability to see company labor relations as a whole. Moreover, plant managers competent in industrial relations are equally important in assuring maximum effectiveness in local union-management relations under a multiplant contract as under single plant contracts.

2. Economic factors

a. The importance of the bargaining issue and the difficulty of negotiation may or may not affect the level of bargaining depending on the ability of the plant manager. However, even a skilled plant negotiator may need more than usual assistance and guidance from headquarters when the subject is a technical one, such as job evaluation, or one that is both technical and involves great expenditures over a long period of time, such as a pension program.

b. A company's bargaining arrangement is affected by the pattern of bargaining in the industry. It is not difficult, for example, for an individual company to maintain single plant bargaining when that is the pattern for the industry as a whole. A multiple industry company may be influenced one way or the other depending on the bargaining patterns and the number of plants the company has in each industry.

c. The location of plants was a frequently mentioned factor. Plants located close together or in areas in which multiplant bargaining predominates are likely themselves to be in a multiplant agreement or parties to a multi-employer regional contract. A number of companies reported a situation in which most of their plants were covered by one contract, while a few scattered ones in different parts of the country remained unorganized or were organized by different unions. Often in such a situation, the chief industrial relations manager negotiates the multiplant agreement, while the plant managers of the scattered plants negotiate their own contracts.

d. An important factor in many companies' willingness to adopt multiplant bargaining or in their highly centralized coordination of local bargaining is bad experience with or the fear of "whipsawing" by the union. It is felt by some companies that whipsawing may force individual plants into an uneconomic wage situation or overload them with fringe benefit costs. Other companies fear that a multiplant bargain may bring such undesirable results even more quickly than whipsawing. It is clear, in any case, that wages and benefits adding substantially to labor costs are subjects so vital to a company that a high degree of centralization invariably exists where they are concerned, whatever the area of bargaining.

3. *The influence of government*

In general the influence of government on union-management relations has been a centralizing one. Many companies stated in earlier studies that the National Labor Relations Board's activities made it difficult to let foremen make final decisions on serious grievances, such as discharge. In this survey, several companies stated "Centralization began early in World War II with the War Labor Board regulations." As plant managers and foremen have become better acquainted with requirements of the National Labor Relations Act and as company decisions and Board decisions have established precedents, less close central supervision has been required. Nevertheless, companies indicated that the central industrial relations department and legal counsel are always alert to any grievances that might involve appeal to a governmental agency, whether the agency be part of the national or of a state government.

4. *Factors related to unionism*

a. The most important factor in the trend towards centralization of responsibility for labor relations—the growth of strong, aggressive unions—has been outside of management's control. Companies generally agree that, when faced by a strong union or unions, top management must be in close control of bargaining, whether negotiating a multiplant contract or a series of single plant contracts.

b. The status of union-management relations at all levels appears to be important in both centralization and decentralization. A factor in management's willingness to bargain on a multiplant basis has been, in a number of cases, a better relationship with the national union than with one or more of the locals. Under these circumstances, management enters a multiplant agreement or, with single plant contracts, works closely with the national officers, hoping that they can exert a rationalizing influence on obstreperous locals. Successful settlement of grievances near the point of origin depends, in contrast, on competent foremen and shop stewards and good relations between them. Upper management's too great stress on friendly relations with the union may create resentment on the part of the foremen just as very friendly union-management relations at a high level may cause some resentment among shop stewards and union members. Greater recognition of common problems and possible common advantages in more substantial delegation to lower levels of management and union would seem to depend on several things: (1) management's willingness to include the union in informal consultation on all matters of interest to the employee-members; (2) a clearer understanding of which issues can and which cannot be settled at the various levels; and (3) what is most difficult of all, a separation of grievance procedures and other plant-local union relationships from the tactical issue of single *vs.* multiplant bargaining.

c. The need for uniformity in industrial relations is recognized by both managements and unions. Managements generally feel that unionization adds to the need for uniformity in industrial relations policies and practices. Whether several unions are competing in a company or one union represents the employees in all of its plants, news spreads quickly and neither union nor management can overlook criticism that one employee or one local is given favored treatment. Moreover, multiplant companies tend to try to maintain equally high industrial relations standards in all plants, whether unionized or non-union. This common acceptance of the desirability of uniform standards and employee expectation of uniformly fair treatment are factors that clearly limit the extent of decentralization.

IMPACT AND CONCLUSIONS

X. THE IMPACT OF THE LEVEL OF DECISION MAKING ON LABOR AND PERSONNEL RELATIONS

ARE there significant differences in satisfactory industrial relations and organizational effectiveness as a result of the policy and practice of centralization or decentralization? This question appears to be of great interest to many American corporations. Unfortunately, the difficulty in finding a clear-cut answer is almost equally great. The evidence in this study that might provide a tentative answer lies in the opinions expressed by the management and union representatives interviewed rather than in any more objective data. However, the relative frequency of certain opinions based on long operating experience has given some basis for their evaluation. Deeper insight into reasons underlying these opinions was gained in the companies in which extended interviews were conducted at the plant level.

A. THE IMPACT ON LABOR RELATIONS

In appraising the impact of centralization or decentralization of decision making on labor relations, the question may be explored from two principal angles. The first is the area of bargaining; the second, the level at which management determines its labor policies and practices. While the two aspects are easily distinguished in certain companies and almost coincide in others, managements generally tend to look upon the level of bargaining as the principal criterion of centralization or decentralization in labor relations, whereas the unions emphasize the location of management decision making.

The previous chapter has shown that policies related to labor relations are nearly always determined by top management. The difference between centralization and decentralization is principally in procedures and application of policies: who negotiates an agreement and where; who interprets agreement or unilaterally determined policy; and at what level grievances are settled. All of these points were considered in discussions with management and unions to determine the effect of more or less centralization.

Attitudes revealed by the 34 companies giving substantial information on the question of the effects of centralization or decentralization on labor relations varied greatly. Half of them felt that there were certain advantages and disadvantages in both centralization and decentralization or that neither was of primary importance to the state of labor relations. Of the 17 companies that saw a marked influence by centralization or decentralization, eleven thought that decentralization was definitely advantageous and six thought the same of centralization.

Most of the companies that saw definitely favorable results either in centralization or decentralization referred explicitly to the area of bargaining. They considered single plant bargaining to be synonymous with decentralization and multiplant bargaining with centralization. Hence the results claimed for single and multiplant bargaining were largely the same as those claimed for decentralization and centralization respectively.

Both unions and managements were asked to compare the effect on labor relations of multiplant agreements and local agreements, and to cite any observed difference in the ease of adjustment to local conditions or in satisfactory day-to-day personnel relationships. An analysis of the replies to such specific questions tends to support the opinion of those companies that saw both advantages and disadvantages in centralized and also in decentralized labor relations and that stressed the greater importance of other factors in more or less satisfactory labor relations.

1. *Company-union relations*

As was reported in the previous chapter, representatives of international unions almost invariably favored multiplant bargaining when they were the chosen representatives of the employees in more than one plant of a given company. When they have achieved the desired unit of bargaining, one point of dispute between the union and company disappears at least from union demands.

Those managements bargaining principally on a multiplant basis generally agreed with union leaders that company-national union relations were better than they had been under single plant bargaining. Some managements felt that improved relations resulted from the fact that the national officers viewed issues less emotionally and more rationally than local officers, and that the former were less subject to political pressures and could give more consideration to the long-run good of the union and its membership. Whatever the points of view of management and union representatives with respect to the desirability of multiplant bargaining, most were inclined to feel that more frequent contacts tended to result in a friendlier, easier relationship between company headquarters and the national office. A few company executives commented, however, that "we still have the same problems."

2. *Relations between plant management and the local union*

Company opinion was divided concerning the authority for industrial relations possessed by plant managers under either single or multiplant bargaining and the effect of the extent of their authority on relations with the local union. Union opinion, generally, was that the plant manager's authority was limited whatever the area of bargaining.

Plant managers themselves felt that they had adequate authority to deal with local issues whether operating under a single or multiplant contract; but most of them also recognized the necessity of a high degree of uniformity in certain policies and of central clearance on all matters that might affect other plants of the company. Some corporation industrial relations executives working in a single plant bargaining situation believed that plant managers would have less authority under multiplant bargaining, and that local plant and local union leadership "matured" more quickly when both were responsible for satisfactory relationships. Most of those with multiplant contracts disagreed, pointing out means of making sure that the plant manager's authority and status were not reduced and the need for referral whatever the type of contract. An exception was the executive of a company that had recently changed to multiplant bargaining who reported the complaint of a number of plant managers that the union now "had the upper hand" and that certain contract provisions had been "forced upon them." Headquarters was not greatly concerned about this, feeling that it was only a temporary reaction to change for which plant supervisors, perhaps, had not been adequately prepared.

Among companies with multiplant bargaining, a few also questioned the premise that day-to-day relations would suffer even if the plant manager had less authority to make final decisions in industrial relations. One executive thought that adherence to certain company policies was more important than any nominal authority possessed by the plant manager. Another executive, expressing a similar point of view, claimed that relations were improved since the union officers knew that the plant manager could act only within agreed-upon policies. A few executives in plants with single plant bargaining suggested that relations with the local union could not be as satisfactory as possible as long as the local officers could complain, with some justification, that they never were permitted to talk with the management people who made the final decisions on important issues.

That the authority of foremen in particular was waning and that this was bad for shop morale was found to be of more frequent concern to industrial relations managers in companies with multiplant bargaining. A few executives referred to the "inside position" of union delegates with respect to negotiations as compared with the difficulty of keeping foremen acquainted with developments. A few managers working with multiplant contracts flatly disagreed with this point of view. They believed that a breakdown in management communications should not be blamed on multiplant bargaining and were firm in their conviction that foreman-steward relations need not be worsened by a master agreement. Several other executives felt that the reduction of foremen's authority was hardly affected by the area of bargaining but, rather, was the result of the growth of union strength in general and the increasing complexity of management organization.

As seen by most of the union leaders interviewed (and on this point national and local officers agreed), the plant manager's authority in industrial relations is always narrowly limited by centrally determined policies and by the general practice of clearing with the headquarters' industrial relations staff on all but the most routine matters. One union representative believed that multiplant bargaining was essential to union strength, but agreed with those management representatives who felt such bargaining tended to weaken both foremen and stewards. The more common union point of view was that foremen have exceedingly small authority in any company, and that it makes little difference whether they are in a plant operating under its own labor contract or as a part of a multiplant contract. Frequent comments were of the following tenor:

"Foremen can't give an answer to anything that is controversial or doubtful. . . . Anything of importance goes to the superintendents' level or to the industrial relations department."

The attitudes of foremen towards the authority they have to handle industrial relations in the shop is one clue as to the effect of the area of bargaining on the foreman. Thirty-one first line foremen were interviewed in five plants with single plant bargaining and nine foremen in two plants covered by a multiplant agreement. (The eighth plant in which interviews were held was non-union.) The latter plants were part of a company that was making a strong effort to get suggestions from all levels of management and to make the plant managers as a group responsible for the labor contract. Taking this particularly favorable background into account, the figures shown in Table 10 are still noteworthy in their indication that the area of bargaining in itself is not a primary factor in giving foremen the authority they feel they need to develop satisfactory industrial relations in the shop.

TABLE 10. FOREMEN OPINION CONCERNING THE ADEQUACY OF
THEIR OWN AUTHORITY AND THE EXTENT TO WHICH THEY ARE CONSULTED

	Of 31 foremen in 5 plants with single plant contracts	Of 9 foremen in 2 plants part of one basic agreement
Satisfied with authority	11 ⎫	6
No objection to fact that authority is limited by need to refer	⎬ 20 9 ⎭	
Would like more authority, or to be consulted more in general or in regard to specified activities	11	3

3. Satisfaction with the handling of grievances

The previous chapter[1] indicated that multiplant bargaining tends to result in the *formal settlement* of grievances at a higher level than is the case under single plant bargaining. However, in matters of discipline and employee grievances, *informal procedures* involving discussion with a higher level than formal procedures would require were found to be important. Companies with multiplant, as well as those with single plant contracts, insisted that it is desirable to have as many grievances as possible settled where they begin. Both union and management expressed concern when many grievances were carried to arbitration.

The chief industrial relations executives of companies with multiplant bargaining tended to emphasize the beneficial effects of a high degree of uniformity in grievance procedures. In their opinion, this largely eliminated complaints of unfairness due to differential treatment. Moreover, the international officers, in a multiplant contract, could keep overly ambitious local leaders from encouraging and enlarging grievances. Practically all of the foremen interviewed recognized the need of a high degree of uniformity in decisions on grievances, but a substantial minority showed a dislike of its attainment at the expense of their own authority or prestige.

Union representatives also stated a preference for the settlement of

[1] Chapter IX, B-3, pp. 159-162.

grievances at the shop level. Nevertheless, in commenting on the fore-man's lack of authority, they also often expressed or implied criticism of management's inconsistency in "pretending" that the foremen handle most grievances when the actual decision is usually made at a higher level.

Satisfaction with respect to the handling of grievances was seen to rest on different bases among top management and the national union executives on the one hand, and the foremen and stewards, on the other. Informal consultation appeared to be the common means of trying to gain a workable compromise between these different points of view. The possibility of a satisfactory settlement of the majority of minor grievances by foremen and shop stewards without resort to the formal procedure was demonstrated in both multiplant and single plant bargaining situations. The evidence from specific plants as well as the variety of management opinion suggests that the area of bargaining is a factor *but need not be the principal determinate of the level* at which grievances are settled or in the *degree of general satisfaction* with griev-ance settlements.

4. *Adjustment to local differences*

Although executives frequently stated that an important advantage of single plant bargaining was the more adequate consideration of local needs, they did not emphasize this fact when discussing the impact of such bargaining. In fact, the majority of company representatives em-phasized the similarities rather than the differences in single plant agreements. It was also found that statements as to areas of differences allowed in single plant agreements negotiated by a given company in-cluded to a large extent those items usually found in supplements to master agreements.

Since one of the companies in which plant interviews were conducted had changed from single to multiplant bargaining about seven years earlier, most of the plant managers and many of the supervisors inter-viewed had had experience under both types of contract. They were asked: Does multiplant bargaining make it more difficult to act in ac-cord with local needs? The response of an overwhelming majority was "No." It was felt that the master contract was written in sufficiently broad terms to allow the supplements to vary according to individual plant problems. The chief factor in assuring adequate attention to local differences was felt to be the way the master contract was currently negotiated. Plant managers were members of the negotiating commit-tee; supervisors were consulted before negotiations began and they were confident that the negotiators now had a genuine concern for local needs.

Evidence that a change in attitude had resulted when plant managers were assigned an active role in negotiations was demonstrated by criticism of the first system of multiplant bargaining. The former method was highly centralized: a headquarters representative "ran the master contract negotiations on his own without consultation with the plant managers" and presented the contract to them as a *fait accompli*. Plant managers agreed that the earlier contracts failed to reflect plant conditions and caused a lot of trouble between plant supervisors and the union. These difficulties, it was claimed, had disappeared when the supervisors were consulted prior to negotiations and the plant managers began to participate in negotiations.

This company's experience gives support to the statement of a number of other companies concerning the importance of negotiated supplementary agreements to the successful application of a master contract. "Off-the-record" agreements, it was reported, often exist between plant management and local union if there is no formal supplementary agreement or if the master contract is too rigid in its requirements for uniformity among the plants covered. Similar "understandings" diverging from announced company policy and the terms of the labor contract were also found in some plants with single plant contracts. Extensive centralization of decisions affecting local conditions appears to breed its own informal balancing mechanism. A few executives with whom this phenomenon was discussed recognized the problems involved. They suggested, however, that the wise manager knew when to challenge and when to overlook understandings that could not be endorsed by the company but might work to the satisfaction of both local management and union.

B. Opinion as to the Effect of Centralization and Decentralization on Intra-Management Relations

1. *Beneficial effects of decentralization*

The outstanding impression gained from a review of management opinion as to the effect of centralization and decentralization on intra-management relations is that all levels of management tend to see what they expect to see. If they are in a company that has stressed decentralization, they tend to see the benefits that have been mentioned as the objectives of decentralization. If they are in a company operating on the basis of a strong central leadership in industrial relations, they tend to think centralization produces the best results.

Thirty-five of the survey companies answered questions concerning the effect of the level of decision making on intra-management relations. Approximately one-third were convinced that extensive delegation of authority improves intra-management relations. These included many of the companies that expressed a philosophy favoring a high degree of decentralization even though their statements as a whole supported the need for a variable balance. Executive opinions as to the effect of decentralization appear to have been influenced in many cases by the company philosophy. The two principal reasons given to support the opinion that the impact of decentralization on intra-management relations was favorable were: (1) that the morale of local management is strengthened with greater freedom to make decisions, and (2) that plant managers and supervisors like to have the right to make decisions even though they do not always exercise it.

An interesting phenomenon related especially to the second point is that members of a given level of supervision almost invariably rated themselves higher in the amount of authority exercised than the next higher level of supervision gave them credit for. The question then is: Do the foremen want more responsibility or only the appearance of more authority than they actually have? This might be the interpretation of the second point and might also be an element in the first— morale. As shown in earlier chapters, the level at which major decisions—even of application of policy—are made suggests that plant supervisors, and even plant managers, are limited in the decisions they personally can make in almost every aspect of industrial relations. And yet they are rarely dissatisfied with the amount of discretion permitted them.

How reconcile the high opinion as to the favorable effects of decentralization on intra-management relations with the real limitations on the supervisors' and plant manager's freedom to make decisions? Part of the answer appears to lie in attitudes, climate of opinion, and the way delegation is handled. Supervisors learn quickly that consultation is essential, and that explicit instructions or the help of an expert in the personnel office is needed in handling or explaining technical matters. Referral becomes a habit. Resentment is felt only when the supervisor or foreman is given no credit for knowing his own men and the facts of a particular situation, or when he is treated in such a way as to lose prestige. Thus there is considerable evidence that the appearance of authority along with recognition of the plant manager's or supervisor's knowledge of local conditions is of more importance in its effect on intra-management relations than the actual degree of decision-making authority delegated and exercised.

2. Beneficial effects of centralization

The principal thesis of the seven companies that saw improvement in intra-management relations under centralization was: a strong central industrial relations department whose role in developing, implementing, and interpreting policies is clearly defined improves the attitudes and cooperativeness of line management. This was felt to be the result of several things: (1) acceptance of the possible impact on the whole company of a decision in one plant; (2) difficulty in keeping a plant supervisor sufficiently well informed to foresee the full impact of his decision; (3) preference for orderliness and "rule by law"; and (4) the psychological strain involved in making important decisions and the desire to share this responsibility with someone at a higher level.

Several of the executives seeing improvement under centralization also were of the opinion that line management is impressed by the fact that top management is interested in human relations. Consequently, supervisors are inclined to seek a greater proficiency in this area. A few also commented that there is better management feeling when the degree of centralization is made clear than when decentralization "is more talked about than practiced."

These companies were among those that favored a high degree of centralization in industrial relations. They considered themselves realistic; and their opinions undoubtedly coincided more with the moderate degree of decentralization found in connection with the industrial relations function in the majority of companies than did the opinions of those stressing the beneficial effects of decentralization. The chief weakness in their point of view lies in its failure to give sufficient weight to the real desire of many managers and supervisors to *feel more independent* and to *take part in the making of decisions* that they have to hand down to the employee. The point made that it is difficult to keep supervisors well informed can be challenged by no one. But it does not lessen the evidence that supervisors want to be kept fully informed and feel that they must be if they are to retain the respect of shop stewards and employees.

3. Relative unimportance of centralization or decentralization

The findings seem to give strongest support to the opinion of the approximately one-half of the 35 companies that the degree of actual delegation of decision making is not of vital importance in intra-management relations. These companies included some leaning towards decentralization as well as some leaning towards centralization. Among them were those who had moved towards more or less decentralization within the past 10 or 15 years. Only a small minority with such experience felt that there was definite evidence that intra-management relations had improved with a change either way. Instead they suggested other factors of more significance in good intra-management relations. Among these factors was the avoidance of a sudden change towards centralization or decentralization without adequate preparation of the management people involved.

The opinion of executives who saw no evidence that a change towards greater centralization or more decentralization had affected intra-management relations was supported by comments of supervisors and foremen. Companies claiming a high degree of decentralization in industrial relations revealed no more satisfaction among their plant managers and supervisors than those companies favoring a substantial degree of centralization. Moreover, differences expressed by supervisors of the same plant and company were much more pronounced than differences among companies. Certain reported experiences indicated especially the need for preparing supervisors for greater responsibility if they are to accept it. In one situation where foremen were resisting increased responsibility for industrial relations, there was a long history of centralization at the department level. In another plant, a former plant manager had turned over all union relations to the plant industrial relations director who was very successful in dealing with the union. The result was a continuing reluctance on the part of foremen to make even minor decisions.

C. Supervisory and Executive Development

A substantial number of companies gave as their reason for preferring a decentralized general management a desire "to develop men faster." Thus the impact of decentralization on supervisory and executive development is of special interest in comparing objectives with results.

Decentralization is considered an important ingredient of supervisory and executive development by just under two-thirds of the 25 companies that commented on this point. Some of these companies believed decentralization to be the most important condition, commenting that, "Delegation of authority is the only way to develop men." An almost equal number of companies in this group stated that decentralization was important but that it was most effective in developing supervisors and executives when accompanied by certain other policies and activities. Among other things mentioned were a policy of promotion-from-within, an established executive and supervisory training program, and a constructive handling of referred questions. Many of these companies also considered delegation of responsibility within each operating unit a more important factor in supervisory and executive development than decentralization extending only to the division or upper plant management.

All but two of the other third of the companies who discussed this question thought the degree of centralization or decentralization had little influence on supervisory growth. Executives in the two companies were of the opinion that centralization was important to executive development insofar as it facilitated the transfer of promotable men and insured a broad training for them. Of the factors considered more important than a policy of decentralization, formal executive and supervisory training and the manner in which superiors and the industrial relations staff handle the referrals made by subordinates were mentioned most frequently. A policy of promotion from within was taken for granted in most of the companies studied.

An executive of one company which stresses decentralization stated that, in his opinion, the centralized executive development program had accomplished more in this field than had the general policy of decentralization. Two-thirds of the companies that considered decentralization to be an important factor already had established, or were initiating on a centralized basis, executive development programs. A few executives pointed out the self-evident fact that such programs are not in conflict with the delegation of responsibility to lower levels of management but that the two activities can go hand-in-hand. In their opinion, even if decentralization does not accompany an executive training program, the development of strong and competent junior executives will eventually encourage greater delegation.

Plant managers and plant industrial relations managers agreed to a large extent with the opinions of headquarters executives as to the importance of the way referrals are handled. Interviews with foremen also gave considerable support to the idea that they must be encouraged *to recommend action* when consulting with their superiors if they are ever to accept more responsibility. The problem is how to maintain a practical balance between learning-through-doing and the risk of seriously bad decisions. Three apparent needs are: (1) to decrease the fear of being reversed, (2) to help the foreman or supervisor make an acceptable decision, and (3) to take the foreman's opinion into account when a decision must be made at a higher level. The methods of upper supervision or of the industrial relations staff in referrals may be more important than who suggests, approves, or hands down a decision. It is clear that the way a referral is handled is a vital factor in developing the self-confidence so essential to willingness and ability to accept responsibility.

D. Employee-Management Relations

1. *General considerations*

The proportion of companies considering decentralization an important factor in good employee-management relations was almost the same as the proportion making a similar response with respect to supervisory and executive growth. Of 28 companies expressing an opinion on this point, 18 felt that decentralization improved employee-management relations, seven felt that the level of decision making was not important, and only three claimed that centralization improved relations more than decentralization. However, the relatively high rating given to decentralization did not stand up as well under close examination as in the case of supervisory and executive development.

The reasons for feeling that decentralization will improve employee-management relations are chiefly associated with the idea of focussing authority at the plant level. This idea is well stated in the following quotation:

"Under our system of decentralization, the local manager has authority and responsibility within himself for the day-to-day decisions of greatest importance in employee relations. He is subject to a framework of company policies, but within that framework he has adequate leeway to handle practically all questions that arise. Because of his own intimate knowledge of the immediate situation and of the people involved, his decisions can carry a far larger measure of justice and effectiveness, in the sense of disposing satisfactorily of the issue or problem, than would ever be possible if the decision-making authority were reserved to a functionary in a central office."

This is a company in which the "framework of company policies" is broader than in the average company studied. Yet with respect to certain activities (college recruiting, supervisor and executive training, the wage structure, pensions, savings, and insurance) policy decisions are completely centralized and application of policy is centralized to a large extent.

Executives of certain other companies expressed their belief in the improvement of employee-management relations under decentralization in terms of goals more than accomplishment. This attitude is illustrated by the following comments:

"There has as yet been no real effort to use decentralization to improve employee-management relations. Top thinking has not yet gone down that far. But in the one division [farthest from headquarters] where the new division head is trying to give more authority to all supervisors you can already see an improvement in supervisor and employee morale."

"Our prime concern is working with the individual. Decentralization is one means to that end. We're not yet satisfied with the results—you can't change ideas overnight."

Those companies that felt that neither centralization nor decentralization was of primary importance in successful employee-management relations emphasized the greater importance of good personal relationships in the shop and the lack of employee interest in the point at which decisions are made. Two companies bargaining on a multiplant basis agreed that good employee-management relations centered in the shop, but they had observed no ill effects on shop relationships as a result of the multiplant contract. One executive expressed the opinion that the centralized bargaining made little difference in employee-foreman relations except to make the employee feel "that he had a stronger union."

Considering the frequency with which discussions with managements and unions brought out the need for a high degree of uniformity in most industrial relations policies, it is of special interest that executives in only three companies stated a strong belief in the more favorable impact of centralization than of decentralization on employee-management relations. These companies contended that uniform treatment of employees resulting from the centralization of major decisions in industrial relations made employees more satisfied that they were all being treated fairly by the company. One industrial relations manager felt also that only through centralization had his company achieved its present high standards in industrial relations, saying:

"It is unlikely that policies would have been established or carried out by plant management without central planning and some pressure upon the plant managers."

Many companies that generally subscribed to the belief that local autonomy is a factor in good employee-management relations agreed that meeting area wage standards, having good benefit programs, and arriving at generally consistent decisions were equally important. A number of executives in these companies, furthermore, considered some restriction of the foreman's freedom necessary to good industrial relations.

The inconsistency between the opinion of a majority of the reporting companies that employee-management relations are improved by decentralization and the extent to which centralized decision making exists in these same companies appears to result, in part, from a tendency to see what is hoped for and, in part, from varying definitions of industrial relations. When discussing decisions on policy or interpretation of policy, even when only one or a few workers are involved, a majority of the executives interviewed recognized the need of a substantial degree of central decision making. However, in discussing employee-management relations, the foreman is seen as the key management figure, and the uniform policies that most of the reporting companies have established recede into the background. Many management people, it appears, tend to minimize the extent of central decision making by emphasizing activities and attitudes that give greater recognition to day-to-day, person-to-person relationships.

2. Employee identification with the corporation or plant

Building and maintaining employee identification with the company is of great interest to most managements that pride themselves on good human relations. Identification with an organization (or loyalty to it) is taken as a sign of high morale and as evidence of good employee-management relations. The question raised was: To what unit of a company organization should loyalty be built?

Employee respect for the foreman was emphasized by many companies. The plant manager, executives sometimes stated, was the highest authority affecting good employee-management relations. Following this reasoning it would seem that the value of decentralization in personnel relations lies in its encouragement and fostering of loyalty to the shop and plant rather than to the division or corporation. The discussion of this question as well as activities in the survey companies, however, showed a division of opinion.

Opinions on this point were secured principally from the plants in which all levels of management were interviewed. Over 80 per cent of the supervisors interviewed identified themselves with the company; the other 20 per cent said they felt their employer to be the plant manager or the division head. Approximately one-sixth of the group made a distinction between their attitude and that of the rank and file, feeling that the latter looked upon themselves as employees of the plant rather than of the division or corporation.

In contrast with the varied opinions of supervisors was the general opinion of high level executives who were seeking greater employee orientation towards the corporation. They felt that employees gain personal satisfaction and reflected prestige in being a part of a large, nationally known company. No corporate officer or industrial relations manager favored employee identification primarily with the plant. A number, however, gave particular reasons why they could not at the moment work towards more widespread employee identification with the corporation. One reason was local collective bargaining. Others referred to historical factors. If, for example, a plant recently purchased by the corporation had good relations with its employees and the community, it was not considered wise to stress the corporation relationship too rapidly.

A considerable number of the responding companies saw no conflict between identification with the corporation and identification with the operating company. As one vice president in charge of personnel expressed it:

> Our goal is to have employees identify themselves with both the plant and the corporation. The relationship between these two must be understood. . . . This identification with the corporation as a whole results from increased advertising by the corporation, by the change in the corporate structure, and from the fact that all the literature has the corporate name printed on it. . . . When corporate officers visit the various plants, they try to point out the security and stability that result from working for the company. . . . Just as one can have loyalty to a state and to the federal government, so one can have loyalty to one's particular plant and to the corporation as a whole.

Nor did companies that emphasized the importance of the authority of the plant manager and supervisor under a policy of decentralization find this policy inconsistent with a preference for identification with the corporation. Such identification, some of them thought, was in fact a result of good local employee-management relations. One personnel director expressed this idea as follows:

> "One of the biggest objectives of the company in decentralizing is to develop close personal relationship between the plant managers and the employees and thereby insure a strong company loyalty which the union cannot alienate."

In this respect, management opinion shows a desire to have the benefits of both centralization and decentralization. Since employees were not interviewed, there was no means of testing the soundness of management opinion. However, to the outside observer there is a possibility of confusion in the effort to build up the employees' acceptance of the final authority of the plant, on the one hand, and to gain the goodwill of employees through uniform policies and practices, on the other.

E. Effect on the Efficiency of the Organization

1. *General considerations*

Only 22 of the 46 companies ventured an opinion concerning the effect of an increased delegation of responsibility for industrial relations on total organizational effectiveness of the plant and the corporation. Of these, ten held the opinion that decentralization improves organizational effectiveness, while only three stated that centralization does. The nine remaining companies thought that neither centralization nor decentralization was an important factor.

Companies that considered decentralization to be most effective thought so for two principal reasons: (1) It was felt that plant officers and supervisors would be more competent and more highly motivated. As discussed earlier, decentralization is considered a major factor in the development of a strong management group. With respect to management motivation, people were said to take a greater interest in their jobs and to be more willing to accept responsibility rather than to shift it. Better employee attitudes, resulting in part from greater respect for local management, are thought to increase productivity. (2) Local decisions were said to be speediest and soundest under decentralization. People close to the situation know more fully what is involved and can make decisions without aggravating time lags.

Centralization was said to have three main advantages over decentralization: (1) it results in lower overhead costs for specialists' services; (2) the application, as well as the determination, of certain industrial relations policies, such as benefit plans, are best centralized; and (3) decisions based on the broader view are generally better than those made from a narrower outlook. Other comments were to the effect that lower overhead results not only because of the most efficient use of specialists but also because expensive training programs and the numerous meetings associated with decentralization are kept to a minimum. It is felt that extreme decentralization tends to confuse the plant managers and to burden them unnecessarily with decisions that must take into account many other plants.

Companies that believed in a reasonable balance between centralization and decentralization of operations or of industrial relations mentioned other factors as the determinants of organizational efficiency. These included: (1) size of the plant; (2) adequate participation in policy determination; (3) clarification of job responsibilities; (4) existence of effective two-way communication; and (5) miscellaneous reasons such as

> ". . . the geographic distribution of the individual plants, the calibre of the resident managements, the nature of the products manufactured, the financial structure of the business, the influences of collective bargaining considerations, and many other factors."

The few companies willing to express an opinion on this point as well as the proportion of those who replied who saw little direct impact from either centralization or decentralization suggests the lack of any extensive or firm conviction as to the effect of the level of decision making in industrial relations on the general efficiency of an organization.

2. Effect on management initiative

Company executives did not often have a strong opinion as to the effect of centralization or decentralization on management initiative. Decentralization, it was frequently stated, increased motivation. Did it, also, they were then asked, increase initiative? The businessmen interviewed generally were more optimistic on this subject than the many writers who have warned against the loss of individuality and initiative and the increasing conformity of thought among management people.

"Just sit in at any management meeting," it was often said, "and see what arguments take place." A few replied, "We know what you mean. When discussion gets past a certain point, we are expected to agree on what is good for the company. But that is essential to any team effort." Most of the men who discussed the effect of decentralization on individual initiative felt that there always must be limitations on differences of opinion and judgment. Conformity to company policy, just as centralization of policy making, is taken for granted. One executive stated:

> "There is a certain quarrel between individual desires and company-wide standards or rules which every company must face. The few congenital nonconformists in industry do not stay long because everyone in modern industry has to accept some regimentation. . . . Conformity need not, however, deaden initiative so long as there is participation by all and so long as the rules are not determined in an autocratic manner and imposed from the top down. Initiative might be diluted . . . but real initiative need not be stunted."

This executive and a number of others contended that a philosophy of decentralization helps reduce the loss of initiative and the pressure to conform. The findings of the study supported this point of view in that companies with such a philosophy appeared to give slightly more recognition to the problem and more effort to a development of conditions that permit the exercise of initiative. Nevertheless, there is evidently a general tendency to underestimate the problem. Variations in local conditions, it was stated, give sufficient area for a fresh approach; encouragement of suggestions and frank criticism, with open channels of communication, provides leeway for the ideas of the younger executives.

A few executives, however, mentioned several angles that worried them. Young executives often are critical of the need to conform, but when promoted to a position where they could encourage more independent thinking they, in turn, demand conformity from their subordinates. A young industrial relations staff member who agreed with this statement was of the opinion that managements were not worried about the lack of initiative since there were enough men who could successfully balance conformity and aggressiveness to fill vacancies in higher managerial jobs. He emphasized the seriousness of industry's failure to utilize the highest abilities of *all* managerial personnel. Another comment was that increasing conformity was a national problem and business institutions were only reflecting national attitudes. Among these few executives it was felt that fear of experimentation and of new ideas in human relations tended to limit especially the delegation of authority for industrial relations and to make a company less flexible in meeting changing social or economic conditions.

In one company, in which plant management was interviewed, headquarters seemed to be more aware of the problem than plant executives. Plant managers expressed no dissatisfaction with the degree to which they could use personal judgment. Headquarters officers saw two problems: the possibility that plant management might develop less ingenuity because of their reliance upon headquarters specialists; and the risk of producing too many "yes-men." In the opinion of the executives of this company management continually faces this dilemma: How encourage initiative and independent thinking and yet keep it within the bounds acceptable to top management?

3. Group and individual decision making

A phenomenon of large organizations related to the question of individual initiative is the extent of group decision making. Many executives have stated that it is often difficult to say just who initiated, or who did determine a policy, and who interpreted it for a given situation. A policy change suggested at a plant managers' meeting, put into writing by the central industrial relations staff, and recommended by a committee representing all the divisions of a company may be extensively modified or accepted without change by the president or by an executive committee. The president, in turn, may announce it as company policy or only recommend its adoption by the subsidiaries. When and how the policy is applied may depend on consultation among several levels of line management and between them and the headquarters and plant industrial relations staffs.

Group decision making is frequently referred to as a characteristic of decentralization, and it was found to be less common in extremely centralized companies than in those with a high degree of decentralization or with a balance between the two. However, every one of the cooperating companies reported some policies established by group decision (through informal or formal discussion), and there was no observable difference in the extent to which it was customary among those seeking a high degree of decentralization and those satisfied with moderate decentralization.

The efficiency of group decision making depends upon the soundness of decisions arrived at, the time and effort involved in reaching a decision, and the effect on the competency of the individual executive. Group decision making, according to a number of executives, assures sound decisions because it allows for the exchange of ideas and takes into account the opinions of those who will be affected by the decision. Group discussion serves also as a means of training.

There were three principal complaints about group decision making. The first of these was the slowness of the process. Although several people mentioned this disadvantage, all but one thought that, by the development of an understanding of the issues involved, decisions were reached which were more likely to endure. The second complaint was that the process consumed the time of too many busy people. A third comment expressed the fear that too many meetings or too much consultation might result in excessive staff influence and might discourage the acceptance of responsibility by individual line supervisors. There must be a limit, it was thought, to the substitution of group or joint decisions for individual decisions. (In one company an employee relations committee had been dropped because of fear of weakening individual acceptance of responsibility.) Union leaders were most critical of the influence of staff on decisions nominally made by a supervisor or plant manager or by committee. A few supervisors also expressed resentiment at the need to consult with the industrial relations staff before making any but the most minor decisions on personnel matters.

In spite of a wide interest in strengthening individual employee-management relationships, group action appears to be increasing within management itself. The point of particular interest is that decentralization, claimed to be a means of giving the individual manager more independence, is characterized by group decision making.

F. General Impression of the Impact of a Greater or Lesser Degree of Centralization and Decentralization

The impact of the unit of bargaining and of a company's philosophy and practice of centralization or decentralization of the industrial relations function was studied with respect to five critical points in good management. These five points were: labor-management relations, intramanagement relations, supervisory and executive development, employee-management relations, and organizational efficiency. In only one —supervisory and executive development—did both reported experience and a majority opinion indicate that either a high degree of centralization or decentralization was of direct importance in assuring satisfaction in these areas. Decentralization (that is, as much delegation of decision making as possible) was seen to be a direct element in the growth of management personnel. But even in this area, a centralized executive development program was felt to be equally important in securing desired results.

The majority of the executives interviewed were of the opinion that a high degree of decentralization was a favorable influence with respect to all five aspects of industrial relations management. However, reports of practice and experience failed to support this markedly favorable rating given to the impact of decentralization. Instead, further discussion brought out that one or several other factors almost always accompanied successful decentralization and that these factors also produced good results where more centralization existed.

These principal factors were found to be: (1) adequate participation by lower levels of management in policy determination and contract negotiations; (2) satisfactory upward and downward communications— especially informal consultation; (3) sound and fair industrial relations policies and plans; and (4) fair and adequate opportunity for promotion. All of these conditions were considered essential elements in effective industrial relations. Yet some of them require more centralization, some more decentralization, and all of them some of both. Decentralization appears to create the more favorable background for communications and participation. Centralization is required to assure high standards in industrial relations throughout a company and company-wide opportunities for promotions. The conclusion is unavoidable that a judicious combination of centralization and decentralization provides the best background for those factors that contribute directly to satisfactory industrial relations.

XI. SUMMARY AND CONCLUSIONS

A. SUMMARY

THIS study of centralization and decentralization of the industrial relations function has included a review of management and union opinion, the extent of decentralization in the industrial relations function, the principal factors influencing the degree of decentralization, and an appraisal of the impact of a greater or lesser degree of decentralization. Throughout the study, discrepancies were found between philosophy and practice and between formal and informal procedures; and basic dilemmas were seen as blocks to managements' efforts to avoid the discrepancies. These discrepancies and dilemmas exist especially in the industrial relations function of management. They would seem also to have more than a little significance for the broader question of the practical extent of decentralization in management as a whole.

1. *Management and union opinion and attitudes towards decentralization*

An overwhelming majority of the chief executives contributing to this study favored decentralized management as a general principle. Industrial relations officers expressed a slightly less favorable attitude towards decentralization, and after interviews involving a review of the levels at which decisions for specific industrial relations activities are made, concluded that for industrial relations as a whole and for most of its sub-functions a variable degree of decentralization exists and is desirable. Moreover, a substantial group of chief executives were of the opinion that the industrial relations function needs a higher degree of centralization than does management as a whole.

The general impression of management attitudes was, thus, one of a strong philosophical preference for decentralization modified to a considerable extent where industrial relations matters are concerned. However, at many points in the study, the philosophical bias towards decentralization appeared to influence the opinions of management personnel as compared with their matter-of-fact reporting of the processes followed in reaching decisions.

Union opinion was, in general, in contrast with management opinion. The union officers interviewed looked upon their objective of company-wide bargaining as a means of correcting the imbalance of union-management bargaining strength now existing when company labor policies are determined at headquarters and negotiations conducted at the plant level. Unions tended to agree with management that minor grievances should be settled as far as possible by shop stewards and foremen. They believe, however, that most foremen have little authority and that informal upward consultation is just another way of attempting to hide the extreme centralization that exists in most companies where union-management relations are involved.

Officers of both international and local unions agreed with management on the need to build up stronger foremen if more authority were to be delegated to them. Only a few union representatives mentioned the possible ill effects of over-centralization within the union. Neither union nor management representatives referred to common problems in efforts to have more decisions made by stewards and foremen, and neither side suggested the possibility or desirability of joint efforts to this end.

2. Location of responsibility for decisions in industrial relations

Industrial relations policies are, with very few exceptions, determined at the corporate level. Implementing procedures also are largely the responsibility of the headquarters industrial relations staff. Even certain decisions in the application of policy to specific situations or persons may be the formal responsibility of a line executive or staff officer at the division or headquarters level. However, the last type of decision is more often the nominal responsibility of the plant manager or a lower level of supervision, although referral to a higher level through informal consultation is not infrequent.

A variety of reasons is involved in the discrepancy between philosophical preference and current practice. Decentralization is sometimes seen as a goal rather than as a description of present procedure. Even with the most sincere effort to implement philosophy, practice inevitably lags far behind. Differences in the definition of decentralization tend to confuse objectives. For example, the state of person-to-person relationships, rather than the extent to which authority for decision making is delegated, may be taken as a measure of decentralization. The conflicting goals of decentralization and of uniformly sound industrial relations in all plants make it difficult for a company to effectuate even the most sincere belief in the value of more extensive delegation of responsibility for industrial relations decisions. And last, decentralization is to some extent a fad, to some extent accepted as a panacea for the problems that have increased with an increase in the size and complexity of industrial organizations.

Whatever the explanation of the discrepancy between philosophy and practice, so far as industrial relations is concerned it appears to be greater today than it was in 1938 or 1947. The companies cooperating in a study of industrial relations administration in 1938 saw the need for greater uniformity and sought to gain such uniformity by making industrial relations a primary responsibility of top management. Marked progress was made towards more uniformity between 1938 and 1947, and few protests were expressed against this centralizing trend.

By 1952 and 1953, when interviews for the current study took place, the popularity of decentralization seems to have obscured the goals of 1938 and the general acceptance of a high degree of centralization in industrial relations in 1947. The philosophy of decentralization had become so pervasive that industrial relations officers in eight companies, in which a comparison of the 1938, 1947, and 1953 studies showed a fluctuating movement with some tendency toward increasing centralization, felt in 1953 that the trend had been towards decentralization or that they had operated with extensive decentralization throughout the 15 years.

The analysis of specific industrial relations activities in 1953 confirmed the impression of the continued high degree of centralization in industrial relations as a whole. It also supported the belief of a majority of the industrial relations officers interviewed that the balance between centralization and decentralization cannot and should not be static. Changes in the level of decision making, for example, were observed in such a commonly decentralized activity as employment, and in such a highly centralized activity as pensions.

3. *Organization, coordination, and control as elements in centralization and decentralization*

Some relationship was found between the corporate functional organization and decentralization of responsibility for industrial relations. When sales and manufacturing are separate major units of an organization, industrial relations policies may be quite distinct between the two, and important decisions may be made at the division level. Also, emphasis in the corporate structure on the unique nature of the division or subsidiary may be an influence towards decentralization to the level in which the uniqueness of the unit is centered.

The strongest influence of organization on the centralization or decentralization of the industrial relations function is the relationship of the industrial relations staff to the line organization. Insofar as the division and plant industrial relations departments have a strong functional relationship to their counterpart at headquarters, the staff influence is centralizing. The extent to which the plant staff feels itself a part of plant management with the responsibility of presenting the local point of view to headquarters is one measure of the decentralizing influence of the plant staff. Within the individual plant, the staff's influence towards more or less decentralization depends mostly upon its informal relations to line management and upon its informal methods of coordinating the application of policies to specific situations.

The need for coordination and control of the industrial relations function is increased by the same factors that exert an influence towards centralization in general. The frequent statement that an increase in decentralization requires a corresponding increase in coordination is further evidence that industrial decentralization is more often a matter of gaining a workable and acceptable balance between centralization and decentralization than a matter of substantial autonomy in the making of important decisions.

Perhaps the most significant finding in coordination is the extent to which reliance is placed on informal referral and consultation. This is true both in the general coordination of industrial relations policies and in the application of specific programs to particular problems. Written material, such as manuals and directives, are standard means of coordination in almost all the cooperating companies, but a majority look upon informal, personal communication as the most vital part of coordination.

Control, in the sense of audit, was found to be more frequently a detailed check on the application of specific policies than a test of the general tenor of industrial relations. This may be due to the fact that no reliable objective measurement of the results of a given personnel or labor policy has yet been devised. The corporate industrial relations staffs were found, with only one exception, to be responsible for such detailed or broader control as was in effect. This responsibility must be kept in mind in assessing the influence of the industrial relations staff towards more or less centralization.

4. Impact of the level of decision making

Opinion concerning the effect of the level at which industrial relations decisions are made varied with respect to the five areas of management considered. Little evidence was found of any relationship between the level of decision making and satisfactory experience in the several areas except in the case of supervisor and executive development. Even in that, the greatest satisfaction with the effect of extensive delegation was reported in those companies where there was a concurrent increased centralization of supervisor and executive training.

A careful check of the opinion of various levels of management as to the impact of the area of bargaining on management-union relations, on satisfaction with the handling of grievances, and on adjustment to local conditions revealed a great diversity of opinion and little evidence of a direct relationship between the area of bargaining and satisfaction in these three matters.

A comparison of foreman satisfaction with their freedom to make decisions or to participate in a decision and with the area of bargaining turned up only one point of interest. Foremen in a plant operating under a multiplant contract expressed more fear of having decisions reversed by higher management than did the foremen in a plant operating under a local contract. In every plant in which interviews were held, however, lower levels of supervision showed some fear of reversal and its possible effect on their prestige, while they also expressed recognition of the need for uniformity in grievance settlements. Informal consultation was found to be the most effective compromise in that particular dilemma.

No significant difference was seen in satisfactory adjustment to local conditions between plants bargaining on a local basis and those that are covered by a multiplant agreement. On the contrary, there was great similarity between the items that vary among the different local contracts of companies bargaining primarily on a single plant basis and those items generally included in supplements to multiplant contracts.

The majority of survey companies were of the opinion that management morale is strengthened by decentralization—even though the supervisor's nominal right to make a decision is not generally exercised. An analysis of the background of this opinion led to the conclusion that maintenance of the prestige of the individual supervisor was desired more than a real increase in responsibility.

Experience seemed to support the common opinion of headquarters and plant managements that delegation and acceptance of greater responsibility in decision making was a significant factor in the development of supervisors and executives. Yet, as in so many facets of centralization and decentralization, the most satisfactory experience was reported where an increase in delegation of decision making was accompanied by a balancing element of centralization—a highly centralized training program which tended to create a uniform approach to the solution of problems. Moreover, in many companies extensive delegation was seen to depend upon upper management's confidence that the persons to whom authority is delegated act on the same principles and assumptions as does upper management itself.

Company representatives also tended to feel that employee-management relations were improved by decentralization. However, managements by no means acted consistently in accord with this belief since most of the survey companies also believed that uniform benefit plans created goodwill for management and that consistency, if not uniformity, was essential in the handling of grievances. Moreover, most of these companies were going to considerable effort to gain employee identification with the company as a whole, rather than primarily with the smaller unit of operations.

5. Factors determining the practical range of decentralization

A majority of chief executives were of the opinion that the industrial relations function in general requires more centralization than operating functions. Reasons for this belief revolve around two principal considerations: (1) acceptance of the idea of an integrated personality of a corporation, especially in management-employee relationships; and (2) the risks inherent in delegation. The first consideration includes such matters as the need for uniform treatment of all employees and the desirability of a common management attitude in the solving of industrial relations problems. The second includes both financial risks and threats to the integrity of the company. Top management, for example, cannot afford to delegate responsibility for such matters as pension plans and general wage changes. The amount of money involved, the risk of serious repercussions from possible inequities, and the need to weigh local considerations against the total company situation are too great.

Centralization also has its limitations. Increase in the size of corporations has put almost unbearable loads on chief executives. Central decisions that fail to take into account variations in local needs or customs have sometimes been ignored by mutual agreement of local management and local union. Recognition of these and other limitations undoubtedly has been an important factor in the recent interest in decentralization, since the move away from centralization has been initiated from the top rather than from lower echelons seeking more responsibility.

Many variable factors determine the practical extent of decentralization for a specific industrial relations activity. The company that seeks to delegate responsibility for decisions in industrial relations must be alert to these factors and their changing impact upon one another. The more important of these variable factors are:

1. Size, number, and location of plants, and their historical relationship to the corporation.
2. The number of industries represented in one corporation.
3. The form of corporate organization.
4. The relations between industrial relations staff and line executives or supervisors.
5. The philosophy, personal characteristics, and ability of key executives.
6. The number of unions, the type of union leadership faced, and the state of union-management relations.
7. The size of the financial commitments involved.
8. The need for the employment of high salaried and technically competent experts.

A serious failure by a management to recognize changing factors which demand a new balance may be offset, in part, by a readjustment which occurs when supervisors passively refuse to follow centrally determined policy, on the one hand, or fail to accept delegated authority, on the other.

6. *Dilemmas*

The need for balance between centralization and decentralization in industrial relations is complicated greatly by certain dilemmas facing management. These dilemmas are numerous and exist in connection with every industrial relations activity. They fall into three principal areas:

(1) The maintenance of the integrity of the corporate personality *vs.* the need for consideration of the uniqueness of the local plants' industrial relations problems.

(2) The great need and desire to use delegation of authority to develop initiative and judgment among lower levels of management *vs.* the pressure of circumstances that strictly limits the possible deviation from established standards and procedures.

(3) The desire to keep collective bargaining to the plant level even when important decisions in both union and management are made at or near the top.

Such dilemmas are inherent both in the difficulties of human adjustment to formal organization and in the multiple goals and responsibilities of industry. They are always difficult and never can be completely resolved. However, the fact that management, in general, tends to over-look their existence makes the approach to a rational compromise all the harder. Insofar as they have been recognized, compromises have been developed on the basis of expediency. Informal rather than formal pro-cedures have provided the essential link between conflicting goals.

B. Conclusions

For many years, one goal in industrial relations management was to make it a responsibility of top management. This goal has been largely achieved and the principle is so strongly supported by the need for company-wide uniformity of policies and their application that even the current enthusiasm for decentralization has affected it little. Important decisions in industrial relations are commonly made at high levels and nothing in this study indicated the likelihood of a reversal of this practice.

Managements' desire for more delegation of decision making is based to a large extent on a dislike of over-centralization and a search for improved structure and administration in increasingly complex indus-trial organizations. The tendency is, however, to overstate the case for decentralization, or to talk decentralization while practicing centraliza-tion. What can management do to clarify its goals and to modify some of the undesirable effects of centralization without losing the desirable and essential central leadership of the corporation's human relations activities?

One point on which there can be no dispute is that there is no panacea for the problems of centralization in large corporations. To present an overall movement towards decentralization as the one solution is to imitate the man, described in the nursery rhyme, who

> ". . . jumped into a bramble bush
> And scratched out both his eyes,
> And when he saw his eyes were out,
> With all his might and main,
> He jumped into another bush
> And scratched them in again."

The problem is immensely complicated, and oversimplification only ob-scures its dimensions. Full fledged decentralization in American in-dustry is no more possible today than for American agriculture to return to the romantic dream of "one acre and a cow."

Nevertheless no corporation can afford to ignore the ill effects of overcentralization and bigness on its human relations problems. The approach must be from many angles and always with consideration of the company's long run as well as its immediate goals in industrial relations. Delegation will then fall into perspective and may be used to best advantage. The formal giving and informal taking back of authority that too often passes for delegation tends often to complicate the particular problem and to prevent a better understanding of the real nature of delegation. The informal and passive resistance to centralized policies that are considered impractical by the local managers may temporarily relieve the strain of overcentralization, but is likely to lead eventually to what one executive called "chaotic decentralization."

Much greater attention to the extent and quality of participation in planning and decision making may prove rewarding. Certainly participation deserves more of a trial than it has yet had in most companies. Participation now often consists principally of communication downward rather than a drawing upward of the constructive ideas of subordinates. Encouragement of independence of expression and a willingness to try out new ideas, and a recognition that each level of management and each individual in it can make a unique contribution may add both to the vitality of the concern and to the satisfaction of its members. It would seem also the only way to develop the "plus value" in delegation that some companies refer to as "a sense of stewardship."

Another point that needs continuous study is the relationship of industrial relations staff to the line organization. Staff, in its purpose and nature, is a centralizing influence. However, the way staff exercises its functional authority may discourage, to the point of destroying, any genuine acceptance of delegated line authority; or it may encourage supervisory self-confidence and the growth of ability to handle whatever responsibility circumstances require. The staff role in developing confidence and competency in decision making among executives and supervisors is as important a factor in modifying centralization as management's ability to delegate. Both are difficult to achieve, but both must be given much more attention if management is ever to develop any effective decentralization in industrial relations.

The chief executives and the industrial relations staff must, it is apparent, work together closely if delegation and participation are to encourage new ideas and the greater utilization of individual abilities and points of view. The trend towards group decision making can result in unthinking conformity to the pattern established by top management, or it can be used to gain wider perspective in modifying the pattern in accord with changing circumstances and to encourage a continual search for an improved pattern. The extent to which management succeeds in encouraging and using each individual to insure sound group decisions may determine the future vitality of industrial leadership and its possible contribution to more enlightened and responsible citizenship.

Appendix A

QUESTIONNAIRE FORMS AND THEIR USE

THE *following basic questionnaire* was used in securing information from the 42 "survey" and 4 "case study" companies. The original form of the questionnaire was pretested by interviews with industrial relations executives in ten companies. Observation of executive reaction to questions, executive comment on the type and form of questions, the adequacy of information received, and the time consumed were all taken into account in revising the original form. In its final form the questionnaire was divided into four parts.

CENTRALIZATION AND DECENTRALIZATION OF THE INDUSTRIAL RELATIONS FUNCTION IN MULTI-PLANT COMPANIES

Company: Date:
Address: Products:
Number of Plants: Number of Employees:
Geographic Distribution:

The following questions suggest the many aspects of centralization and decentralization in the management of industrial relations in the individual company. Supplementary material, such as organization charts, reports of change in form of management organization, or statements of company or executive philosophy with respect to decentralization, as well as your personal comment, will be of interest and value. The term "industrial relations" is used to cover both personnel and labor relations except when one or the other of these is specifically referred to.

Part One. Extent of Centralization or Decentralization of Industrial Relations Organization, Policy-Determination, and Administration

A. Organization
   1. What is the organization of the central industrial relations staff and a typical plant staff? How does it fit into the general organization of the company? (Are organization charts and job descriptions available?)
   2. What is the organizational relationship between the central staff, division or area management, and the plant manager and plant personnel staff? To whom do plant personnel directors report?

B. Policy Development and Determination
   1. What officers or committees are responsible for the formulation of and final decision on changes in principal industrial relations policies or major industrial relations developments? If committees, who are members?
   2. To what extent does plant management participate in the initiation and formulation of industrial relations policies that are ultimately decided upon by central management? Are definite procedures established for consulting with plant management? What role does the central industrial relations staff play in such consultation?

C. Administration
    1. Has there been any formal announcement as to which industrial relations policies may vary from plant to plant and which should be determined and administered by the head office? If no formal statement, is there a commonly accepted practice?
    2. Labor relations
        (1) Multi-plant or single plant contracts? With what unions for majority of employees?
        (2) If negotiations are company-wide, to what extent and by what methods does local management participate?
        (3) If negotiations are on plant basis, to what extent and by what means does central management participate?
    3. At what level and by whom is policy or other change determined and at what level and by whom administered for each of the following? Please indicate also if activity is subject to negotiation with the union.
        (1) Manpower planning
        (2) Employment
        (3) Promotions (non-supervisory)
        (4) Training
        (5) Discharge and layoff
        (6) Wage administration
        (7) Hours of work
        (8) General wage increases
        (9) Vacations, holidays
      (10) Pensions
      (11) Hospitalization and sickness benefits
      (12) Savings and profit sharing
      (13) Grievance procedure
      (14) Arbitration
      (15) Union security
      (16) Health and sanitation
      (17) Safety
      (18) Supervisory training
      (19) Executive development (Are the selection and training programs affected by a policy of decentralization?)
      (20) Time off with or without pay
      (21) Leave of absence

Part Two. Changes in the Degree of Centralization or Decentralization

A. Has your company tended in, say, the past ten years to give more authority to plant managers and plant supervisors or to make more decisions at headquarters? Has there been any difference in this respect betwen matters of general operations and industrial relations policies?
    In your opinion, is it more desirable for your company to maintain industrial relations of uniformly high standards than to delegate more responsibility for industrial relations to plant managers and supervisors?

B. If there has been a marked change,
    (1) What has caused it?
        For example, would you ascribe it to any of the following influences or combination of factors?
        Labor legislation
        Union organization
        Social criticism of "bigness" in industry
        Desire for uniformly "good" employee relations

Increasing size of corporation
Recognition of need for stronger men in middle management
Need for greater specialization in industrial relations
(2) How has the change been received by (a) plant managers? (b) foremen?

Part Three. Methods and Problems in Coordination and Control

A. What methods are used to gain the desired degree of "working together to common ends" in industrial relations in the company as a whole? Within the individual plant? (Executive development, personal visits—how frequent, referral of questions, conferences, personnel policy manual, etc.) Has there been any attempt to evaluate these methods in terms of successful delegation of authority to your plant managers?

B. What controls (such as required approval before action, budgetary limitations, progress reports, etc.) are used by central management or by plant management to assure that established policies are carried out? (Description of specific methods will be of value.) Is success in handling personnel relations a factor in selection for promotion within management?

C. What informal methods of coordination (such as telephone calls, personal exchange of views, etc.) have proved effective? (Comparative extent of use and effectiveness of formal and informal methods.)

D. What do you consider to be the principal obstacles to coordination (poor communications, personnel weaknesses, etc.)? Do they vary from plant to plant?

Part Four. Impact of Degree of Centralization or Decentralization

Have any methods been developed for estimating the effect of an increased delegation of responsibility or increased centralization on:

A. Intra-management relations? (Between head office and plant, and within the individual plant.)

B. Supervisory and executive ability and growth?

C. Employee-management relations? (Within individual departments and plants, and employee attitudes towards the plant and the company as a whole.)

D. Union-management relations? (Please comment on any difference in effect on plant—local union relations and company-national union relations.)

E. Total organizational effectiveness of the plant and the corporation?

If no *methods* of estimating these impacts, what is your opinion of the effect?

Part One of the basic questionnaire was sent to the chief industrial relations officer of selected companies with the request that it be returned with supporting printed material prior to personal interviews. The aim was to secure background data by mail in order to keep interviews to a reasonable time limit and to relate the interview as closely as possible to the particular situation in each cooperating company. The interview afforded an opportunity to obtain more information on subjects inadequately covered in the mailed responses to Part One as well as to cover Parts Two, Three, and Four.

Three hours were found to be necessary for a satisfactory interview. In some cases, the person or persons being interviewed were unable to give three hours of uninterrupted time. Moreover, when two or more company representatives participated in the interview—as happened frequently—discussion of different points of view might consume more than normal time for a single question, reducing the time available for other questions. Since it was difficult, in some of the reports of interviews, to know whether an inadequate report on a given question was due to no clear opinion on the part of the person being interviewed or to lack of time to give explanatory details, the information which did not definitely present the individual's attitude or company practice with respect to a specific sub-function was excluded from the analytical summary.

The companies invited to participate in the survey were chosen from among multiplant companies cooperating on a year-round basis with the Industrial Relations Section. In developing the list, consideration was given to a reasonable distribution by size and industry. The goal was to secure information from at least 25 companies in addition to the ten which had helped in pre-testing the questionnaire. A letter enclosing Part One was sent to 45 companies. A favorable response was received from 35. Three of these were excluded since in each case their several plants were located in one area and industrial relations matters were handled in one central office.

The questionnaire was also used as the basis of interviews with the corporation industrial relations staff and the plant industrial relations staffs in the four case studies. Emphasis in the interviews with line executives at headquarters and divisional levels and with the plant manager was on the broader questions seeking ideas and opinions rather than detailed facts. In the interviews with plant supervisors, direct questions dealt largely with their responsibility for, involvement in, or reaction to the handling of specific industrial relations activities in the plant. The supervisor was told that the study sought to find out who within the plant was responsible for deciding who should be hired, transferred, promoted or "fired"; whether the supervisor was given an opportunity to express his opinion on recently proposed changes in the labor agreement or in company policy or practice, or was kept informed on such developments; and how he felt about the amount of authority and responsibility he had. The supervisors were encouraged to talk about matters—such as grievances—with which they had had much experience and for which, according to their superiors, they were often expected to accept full responsibility.

As had been the experience in previous research projects of the Section, one of the most difficult tasks was finding companies willing to participate as one of the case studies—that is, to permit intensive interviewing at the plant level. The aim was to interview in two or three plants in each of four companies—two of the companies bargaining principally on a single plant basis and two primarily on a multiplant basis. It proved especially difficult to secure the cooperation of two companies with a multiplant bargaining system and with other characteristics sought in the case studies. As a result, in only one case study were the company's principal plants covered by a single contract. In the three other cases, bargaining was wholly or largely on a single plant basis.

The letter to company presidents was as follows:

> Dear ____ _____:
>
> It is essential to the practical value of our study that we have the mature judgment of representative executives concerning the optimum degree of centralization or decentralization in American corporate administration. Your comments on the following questions would be of great help.
>
> Do you favor a higher degree of centralization or decentralization in the general management of your corporation than now exists?
>
> Do you favor more or less centralization of the industrial relations function than of management functions generally?
>
> We should of course be glad to have your discussion of these points. We shall appreciate it also if you will pass on to [industrial relations officer] the enclosed short checklist of questions as to company practice.

The short checklist of questions referred to in the letter sought factual data to provide a basis of comparison between company practice and the chief executive's opinions. The information gained through this short questionnaire also supplemented opinions and data secured by means of the basic questionnaire and personal interviews. Answers to item 7 were particularly helpful in studying the factors affecting the degree of decentralization, and the problems and benefits of a high degree of centralization or decentralization.

CENTRALIZATION AND DECENTRALIZATION OF THE INDUSTRIAL RELATIONS FUNCTION IN MULTI-PLANT COMPANIES

Company:　　　　　　　　　　　　Date:
Address:　　　　　　　　　　　　Products:
　　　　　　　　　　　　　　　　Number of Employees:

1. Are your plant personnel managers primarily responsible to the chief industrial relations executive _____, to the plant manager _____, to some other executive _____?
2. Are major industrial relations policies established on a company-wide basis _____; by each plant _____; sometimes one way and sometimes the other _____?
3. To what extent do plant executives participate in the development of company-wide policies: extensively on most policies _____; extensively on a few policies _____; casually on most policies _____; rarely _____?
4. Is the administration of industrial relations centered principally at headquarters or in the plants?
5. Which of the following are used in the coordination of industrial relations policies in your company?

> Industrial relations manual _____
> Supervisory manual _____
> Regular meetings of plant managers _____
> Regular meetings of all plant industrial relations managers _____
> Regular meetings of plant supervisors
> 　—on a plant-wide basis _____
> 　—on a departmental basis _____
> Visits to plants by the general industrial relations manager _____
> Telephoning between headquarters and plants _____
> Other _____

6. Which of the following are used as means of maintaining desired standards in industrial relations?

      Centralized employment and turnover records   _____

      Centralized setting of salary rates   _____

      Headquarters approval of salary changes above a stated level

        (Please specify _____)   _____

      Approval of plant wage budgets   _____

      Approval of general wage changes   _____

      Approval of promotions below those to plant manager

        (Please specify _____)   _____

      Centralized training

        —for supervisors   _____

        —for executives   _____

      Review of labor agreements   _____

7. What in your opinion, are the principal problems involved in industrial relations administration under a policy of centralization or decentralization?

The questions used as a *basis for interviews with union officers and staff* sought information on the degree of centralization or decentralization within the union, and opinion concerning the effect of the area of bargaining on (1) union-management relations, (2) conflicts of interest among locals and between locals and the international union, and (3) problems of the membership and local leadership. Union opinion was also sought concerning the extent of managements' efforts to delegate and to train foremen "to use their own best judgment in managing their departments, in settling grievances, etc." Finally they were asked, "Have the following items tended to encourage the handling of employee and union relations on a local or a company-wide basis?

    "1. Scientific management, such as job evaluation, time study, personnel departments?

    "2. Labor legislation?

    "3. Size of a company and number of plants?

    "4. Union research staff?"

The opinions collected from unions with respect to (1) the area of bargaining and its impact on union-management relations, (2) the extent of managements' efforts to delegate, and (3) factors that encourage more or less centralization were reported in Chapters IX and X of the preceding report. Findings concerned particularly with intra-union relationships and their impact on the level of union decision making in collective bargaining will be discussed in a short supplementary report.

Appendix B

METHODS AND PROBLEMS IN ANALYSIS

A DIFFICULT problem in the analysis of first-hand information concerning industrial relations management is how to reduce it to quantifiable data or, at least, to a basis permitting comparisons among companies and among activities. It is essential, also, to identify the most significant variable elements in each subject area. The number of variations in opinion and practice and the difficulty of classification increase with the amount of information. The bulk of material gained through two different questionnaires, a letter seeking the opinions of chief executives, and a total of 293 personal interviews, plus supplementary printed material from companies and unions, presented unusual difficulties.

The interviews did not seek yes or no answers or even short statements of "usual" practice, since it was found early in the pretesting of the first questionnaire that first short statements tended to be generalizations supporting what was presumably company philosophy. Rather, the persons being interviewed were encouraged to give detailed descriptions of procedure in specific cases, thus bringing out the variables that had affected different procedures for the same activity and similar problems at different times or in different units of operation.

Judgment and attitudes were involved throughout, both on the part of the research team and of the company and union representatives. An effort was made to classify the information received so that it could be used quantitatively. However, much of the information could not be reduced to quantifiable data. Moreover, few of the statistical summaries could stand on their own but had to be weighed in the light of the pertinent background and modifying factors.

It is interesting that the most easily quantifiable information was that which was wholly opinion. Statements of fact, describing procedures or reporting experience, showed so many variables or were so evidently influenced by the attitude of the interviewee that the analyst had to exercise considerable judgment in classifying and interpreting them. For example, replies to the letters to presidents were easily classified into three groups; but experimentation with several methods was necessary before reaching an acceptable means of determining a general or normal level of effective decision making for a specific industrial relations activity in a given company.

The responses to the short questionnaire also were easily quantifiable but they gave comparatively little insight into the relative force or depth of centralization or decentralization in a specific company. A question, for example, that asked which of seven methods were "used in the coordination of industrial relations policies in your company" gave a picture of the extent to which these various methods were used but provided no insight into problems involved in their use nor the extent to which companies relied upon them as means of coordination.

Even the fuller answers received by mail to C-3 of Part One (asking at what management level and by whom policy was determined and administered for each of 21 activities) were so general that, if they had not been supplemented by personal discussion, a highly inaccurate picture of the levels of decision making would have resulted. The additional details showed the variables that had to be evaluated in determining the effective level of decision making and prevented grossly oversimplified conclusions.

Three methods were tested in attempting to establish the extent of centralization or decentralization of a single industrial relations activity in a given company. A "code" for analysis included eight points showing different authority for, or types of influence exerted on, policy decision and decisions in the application of policy. These ranged from reporting to a superior *after* a decision was made to formal and direct responsibility for a decision. This code was used on an analysis sheet on which all levels of management from the board of directors down to foremen were listed.

One member of the research team based his rating of each activity as "centralized" or "decentralized" according to the location of the highest point at which a formal decision was made or to which the question was referred before a decision was reached. Another used the same analysis sheets but, independently, also reviewed all the information on the one activity from each company and, on the basis of the most common practice— considering both formal and informal procedures—in determining, implementing, and applying policy, rated the activity as principally centralized or principally decentralized. The third member reviewed the material and, without reference to the analysis sheets, recorded his impression of whether the activity in each company was principally centralized or decentralized.

The greatest difference in the ratings was between the one based on the highest point of referral or decision making and the two in which the analyst's judgment was involved to a greater degree. The first method tended to show much more centralization than the other two. Ratings differed substantially between the second and third raters only in the case of seven out of 46 companies. These two raters then discussed the basis for their ratings and arrived at a mutually acceptable rating of specific activities and company classification.

The companies were divided into three classes: highly centralized, balanced, and highly decentralized. The criteria for these classes were as follows:

Highly centralized. Corporation or division headquarters formulates or negotiates and adopts policy, issues notice of decision, develops procedures, and sometimes makes the effective decision in the application of policy in *at least two-thirds* of the activities considered a part of the industrial relations function.

Balanced between highly centralized and highly decentralized. Plant management may make certain decisions on policy, frequently develops implementing procedures, and generally is fully responsible for the application of policy in the case of *more than one-third but less than two-thirds* of the activities in industrial relations. Plant management was given credit for making a decision even though it was common practice to consult informally with headquarters prior to making decisions that might have an impact on other plants.

Highly decentralized. In companies thus classified, the plant management generally makes decisions on policies as well as being fully responsible for their implementation and application in the case of at least two-thirds of the industrial relations activities. As in the "balanced" group, plant management may consult headquarters informally before making decisions that might affect other plants of the company, or, as a minimum, keeps headquarters regularly informed of industrial relations developments.

The classification of the companies, as described above, was done as systematically as possible by each of the three researchers working on the analysis of material. Results of the one method that indicated some bias towards centralization were discarded. The final classification, if biased either way, favored decentralization. The results (25 highly centralized, 19 balanced, and 2 highly decentralized) were all the more noteworthy in their contrast with company philosophy.

INDEX

OTHER PUBLICATIONS OF THE INDUSTRIAL RELATIONS SECTION

Reports

Hiring Practices and Labor Competition. Report Series No. 88. 1954. 108 pp. $2.50.
Centralization and Decentralization in Industrial Relations. Report Series No. 87. 1954. 218 pp. $4.00.
Retirement Procedures under Compulsory and Flexible Retirement Policies. Report Series No. 86. 1952. 65 pp. $2.00.
Compulsory Arbitration of Utility Disputes in New Jersey and Pennsylvania. Report Series No. 85. 1951. 90 pp. $2.00.
The Operation of Sickness Benefit Plans in Collective Bargaining. Report Series No. 84. 1951. 109 pp. $2.50.
Maximum Utilization of Employed Manpower. A check list of company practice. Report Series No. 83 (Revised) 1951. 54 pp. and 4 p. check list. $1.00.
Layoff Policies and Practices. Recent experience under collective bargaining. Report Series No. 82. 1950. 55 pp. $2.00.
Personnel Administration and Labor Relations in Department Stores. An analysis of developments and practices. Report Series No. 81. 1950. 144 pp. Paper bound $2.50; Cloth bound $3.00.
Job Modifications under Collective Bargaining. A survey of company experience and four case studies. Report Series No. 80. 1950. 77 pp. $2.00.
Transmitting Information through Management and Union Channels. Two case studies. Report Series No. 79. 1949. 141 pp. Paper bound $2.50; Cloth bound $3.00.
Company-wide Understanding of Industrial Relations Policies. A study in communications. Report Series No. 78. 1948. 78 pp. $2.00.
Company Wage Policies. A survey of patterns and experience. Report Series No. 77. 1948. 45 pp. $1.50.
Management Procedures in the Determination of Industrial Relations Policies. Report Series No. 76. 1948. 81 pp. $2.00.
Constructive Labor Relations. Experience in four firms. Report Series No. 75. 1948. 116 pp. $2.00.
The Operation of Job Evaluation Plans. Report Series No. 74. 1947. 111 pp. $1.50.
Wages under National and Regional Collective Bargaining. Experience in seven industries. Report Series No. 73. 1946. 103 pp. $1.50.
Group Health Insurance and Sickness Benefit Plans in Collective Bargaining. Report Series No. 72. 1945. 89 pp. and charts. $1.50.

Bibliographies

Industrial Pensions and Retirement Procedures. Bibliographical Series No. 82. August, 1954. 24 pp. 50 cents.
The Office Library of an Industrial Relations Executive. Bibliographical Series No. 81. (Revised) July, 1951. 48 pp. $1.00.
A Trade Union Library. Bibliographical Series No. 80. (Revised) June, 1949. 54 pp. 75 cents.

Subject Index of the Library of the Industrial Relations Section. (Revised) November, 1951. 62 pp. $2.00.

Complete list of available publications will be sent on request.